Published in Great Britain and the United States of America in 2017 by
CASEMATE PUBLISHERS
The Old Music Hall, 106–108 Cowley Road, Oxford OX4 1JE, UK
and
1950 Lawrence Road, Havertown, PA 19083, US

Hardcover Edition: ISBN 978-1-61200-550-8
Digital Edition: ISBN 978-1-61200-551-5

A CIP record for this book is available from the British Library

Printed in the United Kingdom by TJ International Ltd

For a complete list of Casemate titles, please contact:

CASEMATE PUBLISHERS (US)
Telephone (610) 853-9131
Fax (610) 853-9146
Email: casemate@casematepublishers.com
www.casematepublishers.com

CASEMATE PUBLISHERS (UK)
Telephone (01865) 241249
Email: casemate-uk@casematepublishers.co.uk
www.casematepublishers.co.uk

Maps are based on originals from J. Canaud and J.-F. Bazin: *La Bourgogne dans la seconde guerre mondiale*, Le Grand souvenir (Ouest France: 1986).

In memory of "Louis" and those whose blood was spilled in my native Morvan.

Forewords

Colonel Maurice James Buckmaster

Chief of the French section of Special Operations Executive

Events of around 30 years ago are still vivid in the memories of those of us who lived through them, but for new generations, Hubert Verneret's war diary will be a very moving and very precious story about the actions of the Resistance during the Second World War.

I like to think that the Franco-British co-operation of that period plays a part in tightening the cordial bonds which connect us.

I also like to think that the personal friendships forged in the fire of combat will bear fruit at the end of these 30 years, and that the spirit of camaraderie born on the battlefields, in the forests and in the camps, will prevail over the disputes that inevitably divide politicians on both sides.

Hubert Verneret was able to highlight the feelings of young people of his time; they match our memories exactly, whether we lived in France or in Great Britain, whether we were then wearing His Majesty's uniform, or the armbands of the maquisards.

I am very proud to have been able to take part, albeit in a minor way, in the Liberation of France, and to be able to join in France or welcome at home, friends of olden times who are also friends of today, whilst saluting the memory of those who died on the field of honour.

Maurice James Buckmaster
London, 1971

Colonel Jean d'Escrienne

Aide-de-camp to General Charles de Gaulle

When I arrived in England, in early 1942, after a clandestine trip across Spain and Portugal, the Allied war machine was not yet developed, and Hitler was triumphant everywhere. The British, however, just like General de Gaulle, had no doubt about the victorious outcome of the conflict, even if they knew perfectly well that it was a long way off.

Concerned, therefore, about future fighting on French soil, the British secret services, as well as those of the Free French, did not hesitate to question me at length about the Nièvre, and more especially about the Sud (South) Morvan. It was not difficult for me to show them, using a map, the opportunities and the benefits of our topography and landscape, conducive to camouflage and to clandestine organisation and actions.

I was also asked the names and addresses of French people living in the region, whom the Allies could trust when the need arose. Of course, I first gave the name of my mother who lived permanently on our Lavault property near Millay.

Many months, however, were to elapse before the creation of the Louis Maquis and its setting up at Les Fréchots camp. My mother actually had various contacts. She was even visited by Colonel Buckmaster. Having received no news from her son in the Free French Forces for more than 2 years, unaware of where he could be fighting, and even whether he were still alive, it was with pleasure that she also volunteered to serve.

Lavault therefore became the meeting point for "Louis" (Paul Sarrette) and others resisting in the region and also from further afield. Thus, upon his arrival in March 1944, Kenneth Mackenzie (Captain "Baptist") was hosted in Lavault. The radio transmitter that allowed him to communicate with London was hidden in the house, and then in beds of hydrangeas around the park, including behind the statue of Our Lady of Lourdes, which my great-uncle had erected in the aftermath of the First World War.

I only had knowledge of this later when I came back on leave in December 1944, after three years spent out of France. The Louis Maquis had then ceased to exist. I learned about the roles played by some I had known before the war. I met Captain Mackenzie, whom I saw several times subsequently, and who returned every year on pilgrimage to our region. He never failed, on these occasions, to go and put flowers on my mother's grave, after she had left us.

It is fair to salute the attitude of all those who came to the Fréchots, even those who did not take part in any combat. Their attitude was a refusal. It showed, indeed, a refusal to submit, to work for the enemy, to go and work in his country – in a word, it was the refusal to collaborate.

Thus, when it was time for the last fight, the fight for Liberation, maquisards and resistants vindicated once again the great solitary voice who claimed in London on 18 June 1940, in a speech both grandiose and tragic: "The flame of the French Resistance must not be extinguished, and will not be extinguished."

As time passes, witnesses pass away, and emerging generations tend to forget experiences. It is why, before leaving this world, those who have lived through great moments of our history have the duty to remember them so that the glories of yesterday are a subject of pride and hope for the generations of tomorrow.

Jean d'Escrienne
Lavault, 7 January 2008

Contents

Part I: Hubert Verneret's Diary

Introduction

I haven't opened this diary in 25 years and I confess to being unable to browse through it without some emotion.

One always discovers with surprise the young person one was, a young person struck by things basic and true.

As we age, the scales may fall from our eyes, but our vision is distorted by magnifying glasses that alter the truth. Pity the butterfly that believes itself more evolved with its multifaceted eyes, than the robust caterpillar in its cocoon!

I think that children get to the heart of things differently, as they are in harmony with them; they are on the same wavelength and travel on paths free from memories, paths not yet cluttered with thoughts and analyses.

What strikes me in my story is to find in almost all events some thoughts of a student only recently out of his last philosophy course!

I will not therefore deny the teenager who would have preferred to own a machine gun instead of a rifle, no doubt to kill more Germans; and had noticed that his captain's table was often graced by a small vase of wild flowers. I rather wonder whether the "man" I became, 25 years later, would still be willing to fight. The past is no guarantee of the future, nor can the sun of yesterday really warm you up when it rains on your town or in your heart!

H.V.

Left: Hubert Verneret in 1945, at the time where he transcribed his notes written, often in haste, whilst with the Louis Maquis. Right: Hubert Verneret in 2017.

1938

13 years old

11 March

Adolph [sic] Hitler chose my birthday to invade Austria!

I heard my father say to our neighbour: "This is serious, it could very well lead us into war."

20 August

Green Auvergne, dark and mossy, lit by the flames of our campfire on your extinct volcanoes, silent and deep Auvergne enlivened by the shouts of our games, how I love you!

This is the first time I have seen a mountain; what a wonderful camp! Usually, our Scout groups camp around Nevers, or on the edge of the department of the Côte-d'Or. This time the fundraising fete must have been particularly successful, for the leader to take us at least 250km away from Nevers.

I would be completely happy if only the business of the thief did not keep coming to mind. René announced earlier, at the meeting of "patrols" before dinner: "Tonight you will have to take turns on guard, because strangely, somebody tried to burgle our supplies. The Scout leaders chased a bearded man this afternoon, but alas, did not catch him."

The campfire was great. René told a stunning Arab story. He really has an extraordinary accent: what a gift for imitation.

I suddenly realise that each tent is a good hundred metres from the next, and we're in the middle of the forest! René added: "You will take your stick, a whistle, and I will lend you my big flashlight, but you must only turn it on in an emergency."

Our patrol presented a sketch about snail gathering.

At what time will I stand guard? Why doesn't René want us do it as a twosome?

The "Beavers" patrol mimed "Perrine was a servant". Their mimes are always excellent.

The last flames die. After praying together, René announces in a cheerful voice: "And now, everyone to their tents, I've tortured you enough with this far-fetched gangster story." Was it true? Or did he only want to reassure us?

The older Scouts did say that on every camp there was a scare story. So?

Meanwhile, I am the happiest of Scouts: I have escaped guard duty, which, I admit, had somehow made me feel extremely anxious.

War ... What is it like? Is one afraid, really afraid?

1939

14 years old

1 September

Hitler has given his senseless order. The Germans have invaded Poland. How dreadful! Everywhere they are saying that this will be war.

3 September

This is it, France is going to the rescue of the Polish. In the street, women cry.

4 September

I stayed for a long time in front of the poster ordering general mobilisation, and then I put my Boy Scouts' uniform on before going to the train station to meet refugees[1] who are already arriving with their huge suitcases. We help them to join their families or find an accommodation centre.

5 September

For the moment, it is rather exhilarating. Some teachers have not yet been replaced; they will doubtless be replaced by old men who will be less strict. There will surely be changes at the school. It would seem that the Headmaster himself is on his way to a gunpowder factory, where he will fill shells with explosives. I honestly can't say that I am sad, nor can I intone with the adults: "What a tragedy!"

There are those from the First World War, who tell hair-raising stories, but they have such a way of adding a little cheerful note to their stories after the heroic verse, that in the end you wonder whether they are not watching the

---

[1]Border areas in Eastern France were evacuated early on in the war.

others leave with, perhaps, a certain nostalgia. Are they thinking of their long gone youth?

After school, I went down to the station. A train full of soldiers had stopped near the bridge at Fourchambault. Hanging out of the doors of their cattle trucks, they were singing at the tops of their voices. What confidence! I am sure that these men will soon be marching victorious through German cities.

It was only later, when I was alone in my bed, that it occurred to me that many of them would perhaps die. So then why were they singing: "This is only goodbye, my brothers, yes, we'll meet again"?

6–8 September

As soon as I have a free moment, I go and join the other Scouts of my patrol at the station. We meet there day and night; there is always a single old man, hanging onto a heavy burden like flotsam, and waiting; or a woman surrounded by dirty children, lost, frightened or asleep.

We greet a joyless crowd with no young men. The very young and the old leaning on one another, and it is up to us to reassure, to guide. Clément said to me yesterday: "When I find a suitcase is too heavy, I think of all the treasured objects that they had to leave behind!" How true.

The first air raid warning took us by surprise at the station, at dusk. What a panic among the refugees. However, we had to reassure them, with our own fear well hidden inside!

10 September

We were called into the station manager's office. It is thought that spies are monitoring the movements of our troops. They wear French uniforms, but the number of their regiment, hidden as it should be in time of war under the regulatory tab which folds onto the collar of the jacket, does not match up with that of any regiment due to enter Nevers Station. Up to us to unmask them! It is child's play to cheekily lift the small band of khaki cloth, looking the picture of innocence, to discover the number that it conceals. But alas, we find no spy!

October

The influx of refugees has passed. We have settled into war. The Scouts now assume various tasks; I am liaison agent, and in case of alarm, I have to leave my school bench or my bed at once, and cycle to the gendarmerie.

I have made myself a pass on a piece of a white card found in one of my father's desk drawers.

I write: "I certify that the Scout Hubert Verneret, in case of alarm, must report to the gendarmerie of Nevers". Then I had it stamped twice: once by the Commander of the gendarmerie, and once by my Scout patrol leader.

Now I can prove to the dear monk that instead of going down with other students to the shelter deep in the cellars of Saint-Joseph School, I must, at the first wail of a siren, leave my comrades. I admit that I do it every time with a certain joy, and an enormous sense of superiority!

I do nothing at the gendarmerie, but I am in the open air. The gendarmes are equipped with boots, helmets, and are ready to intervene in the event of bombing or paratroopers. As for me, I'm in sandals and my head is bare whilst I take part in this prodigious production.

I have no gas mask either, as I realised to my discomfort a little while later. After many false alarms, a German plane had dropped a string of bombs on Nevers. One small one fell on the gendarmerie, and a terrible smell began to emerge. A few minutes later, I had a pathetic handkerchief wedged under my nose, while around me the regulation masks had transformed the gendarmes on guard duty into Martians. Fortunately, the asphyxiating gas was pretty harmless, and came from a quiet place where we love to withdraw alone at certain hours of the day! I knew, however, from this moment, that in life, one should not rely too much on others, and consider only one's own survival.

1940

15 years old

June

Our troops are retreating, but I am confident in the final victory. In 1914, didn't "they" reach the gates of Paris! Refugees begin to pass through again, but this time the flow is huge. In entire trainloads and on the roads, the French have taken over from the Belgians and Luxembourgers. All we see are cars overloaded to the limits of their possibilities, which go by day and night, forming a huge, sad and hungry river.

The Germans are in Orléans! The real debacle has begun. For fear of the invader, everything with wheels has hit the road: remember the atrocities committed during the previous war. It all moves at walking speed; cars running out of petrol are pushed into the ditch, and the progression of the slow metal snake continues, from one alarm to the next, with three cars running abreast. It is a one-way route of flight and fear!

In the evening at home, we take in exhausted refugees, thinking that tomorrow, perhaps, it will be our turn. We will swell the flow.

Papa has set aside the necessary petrol. We have already discussed amongst ourselves a possible destination. It is clear that we must leave. If fighting should start, this could only be on the Loire River, and more precisely in Nevers. My parents are thinking of going to the countryside. It is not necessary to go far to be safe. But we must leave Nevers if German pressure increases. There is no option.

I go to the station almost day and night. I'm exhausted. The station doors are closed. Why would one let people enter without being sure that one can evacuate them? Thanks to my uniform and a safe-conduct, I can enter without difficulty, and find inside this bedlam a huge, hungry crowd, fighting to find a place, even in a corridor, each time there is a train. How many abandon their precious suitcases on the platform, so as to be able to climb on board?

Everywhere drama erupts; families are separated, children are crying, wounded men moan. There are no more supplies at the shelter, and they are short of drugs at the makeshift infirmary set up within the walls of the station.

Our soldiers are now in complete rout, and turn up, sometimes unarmed, amongst the flood of refugees. A black man in uniform, who has come from La Charité-sur-Loire, asks me where to spend the night. I take him to our Scout building, on the Rue Adam Billault. Along the way, he tells me that we are hopelessly lost; spies are everywhere in vulnerable places, and our aeroplanes are only to be seen on the news at the cinema. What can be done without weapons and ammunition? Yet he, son of Africa, expresses his readiness to die for France, even though our behaviour towards Blacks, he says, is not always exemplary. Maybe France deserves a punishment, he adds.

France deserves a punishment? This idea, which has never crossed my mind, seems monstrous!

For a long while, I listen to him. He speaks an impeccable, indeed sophisticated French. He speaks to me as if I were an adult man, with friendship and respect, and I can't believe that so much intelligence, goodwill and love can find themselves helpless in a shabby building, with an exhausted boy for an audience.

That night, I understood that skin colour was only apparent, and that there were only men happy to be together, or unhappy to be together.

15 June

The situation is really precarious. My parents are taking all necessary steps to leave Nevers tomorrow.

16 June – Sunday

A Sunday unlike any other. I have an appointment with Clément to go to 8 o'clock mass at Saint-Étienne, but there is no mass! There will be no mass today. Is this conceivable? As we are in uniform – we almost never take it off – we go straight to the station. The large courtyard outside is literally invaded by the people of the Nevers region who want to flee. We manage, not without difficulty, to reach the Reception Centre, where we find Roger Weber, Parisian scoutmaster and military doctor. He tells us that all resistance is now out of the question, even on the Loire.

With two nurses from the Red Cross, we begin to distribute the last of the food, when a gentleman takes the two nurses to one side, and says to them: "Come quickly, we are leaving now."

This is how Clément and I become heads of the Reception Centre on this Sunday morning of 16 June 1940. But a short time later, we too have to abandon our posts.

Shortly before 11 a.m., Roger makes an appearance once again. "Go onto the platform. I need you both: a hospital train is due to arrive at any moment. A lot of wounded men have just been brought in, and we must load them. First of all, give them a drink, and then clear a path along the platform, if possible over a metre or a metre and a half width."

Meanwhile, two new nurses have come to help us. These two will stay.

We go into the hall adjacent to the Reception Centre. On rows of stretchers side by side are lying wounded soldiers. What a sight! All that coagulated blood staining the dressings, all that blood that continues to flow. It is the first time that we have seen wounded soldiers. We are alone with them. Awkwardly, we try to give them something to drink.

I have the feeling that these men are children: a look begging for a little water, an arm reaching out. We need to be with all of them at the same time. What on earth can we do facing these beaten men, facing these lives that are ebbing slowly away?

How I would like to forget these two eyes watching me, half supported by prayer, half-dazed with pain. What is a dying soldier thinking about? Because he is dying, I am sure. In a few moments, perhaps.

Now we must go and ask refugees to clear the edge of the platform as the train is about to arrive. It's impossible to get the crowd to co-operate. We have to get out our Scout's penknives and poke people with the blade in order to carve a narrow corridor with great difficulty. Roger joins us just as the train enters the station.

Loading of the wounded begins at once. The soldier with the head wound gives his last gasp just as he is hoisted into the carriage. Roger orders that we take him back down onto the platform. He is taken to the hall where Mademoiselle du Verne closes his eyes. Stretcher after stretcher. How long does it last?

I finally get home to the Rue Dupin where my anxious parents are waiting for me so that we can leave. I explain in a few sentences. My expression would have sufficed.

We have two cars: ours, and that of a cousin who can't drive and whose husband has been mobilised. Papa immediately leaves the house with the first car; he has tied his bicycle behind the boot, in order to come back later and get the other car.[2] My sister, who does not have her driving licence either,

---

[2] My father, who had served 7 years in the armed forces at the time of the First World War – if we include 2 years in the regiment and 1 year of occupation duties – could no longer be called up.

will drive it anyway, when the tricky part of the route has been negotiated. We will take small secondary roads, in an attempt to reach Cercy-la-Tour, our first stop.

Night is about to fall when Papa finally joins us. He is on foot! When he arrived at Saint-Éloi, he found that his bike had been completely wrecked by cars that were following him. We leave soon. I am on a bicycle. How will my father try and get through this time? Through the suburbs of Mouesse? This seems impossible. So, will we have to go upstream through the side streets, then try to cross the flow, reach Trangy and from there Saint-Éloi?

We are blocked for several hours before we can clear a passage between two rows of cars. We finally reach the cemetery. We run into a military convoy. The trucks carry large metal boats. The soldiers no longer have officers with them. Were they killed? Have they left? They consider taking up a position on the Loire. Good luck to them!

A van manages to manoeuvre against the flow towards Coulanges. Papa drives in its wake, followed by a Belgian car. On my bike, I can follow easily, despite the total darkness. We end up on a small deserted road. Now, we need to cross the Loire, quickly. But where? At Decize? At Bourbon? Crossing the Loire: this phrase is on everyone's lips. On the other side of the river, it would seem that we will all be safe.

Suddenly, we see a car in the ditch. Papa stops. A woman and eight children are trapped inside, shouting and crying. Fortunately, no one is injured. As the people in the van and the Belgians have also stopped, together we can quickly push the car back onto the road.

A kilometre further on, it is my turn to be in distress because of a flat tyre. As I am bringing up the rear, I must act quickly. I take my whistle and call for help: immediately, the cars speed up. I whistle again: this time, they stop. Phew!

Obviously, the Germans are nearby. But my father remembered in the nick of time that he had a son!

It is out of the question to do the puncture repair on the spot, in the dark. The Belgians take me with them, and my bicycle is tied somehow onto one of the cars. Let's hope that it will be luckier than Papa's. I have had a puncture only once in 3 years, and it had to be today!

Shortly before Cercy-la-Tour, my sister misses the exit of a chicane set up on the road by soldiers and drives her car slowly but surely into the ditch. Maman, climbing out, falls into a nettle patch. She gets up crying. Everyone's nerves have been on edge for days.

Two men are sleeping nearby, in the ditch. We wake them up, and together put the car back on the road, not without difficulty.

Another few kilometres and we arrive at grandmother's place. How could we have guessed that we would find the door closed? Being afraid of the

Germans, at her age, in a small village of a few thousand inhabitants, and, what is more, tucked away from the main roads, it really doesn't seem like grandmother! I would more easily have imagined her standing up to a section of German paratroopers, alone. Something must be happening, but how can we find out?

A woman comes in with her child in her arms. She shouts: "A doctor! A doctor!"

A cyclist stops near us: "The Germans are less than 20 kilometres away," he says.

How are we to decide? Why not go to Crécy-sur-Somme with our cousin, and stay with relatives we have in common? The low fuel tanks decide matters. We must go to Crécy, to the Hôtel du Cheval Blanc.

We finally arrive, one car towing the other, for it is out of petrol.

According to my mother, I must immediately remove my Scouts' uniform, in order to "welcome" the German troops without causing further trouble.

The Wehrmacht doesn't keep us waiting. First to arrive are two motorcyclists in black raincoats, with machine guns wedged on their stomachs. They stop at the Hôtel du Cheval Blanc to open champagne. They drink to our health, with the satisfied look of tired victors.

Maman had to hide my sister in the back kitchen, for at 19, she must not be present as the first occupants arrive!

End of June

After the lines of armoured vehicles and their stream of accompanying supply trucks had gone past, calm finally returned. A week later, it seemed that the Germans had left France.

Then Papa returned to Nevers on my bicycle, in order to feel the temperature of the water. A much admired performance!

"Uncle is still in good shape," I heard people saying around me, and I was very proud to be the son of "Uncle".

Our house was not requisitioned; we could therefore return to it when we chose to, which we did in the days that followed.

2 July

Nevers is occupied. How sad! I fully understand, this time, the meaning of the word "defeat".

In the town, which looks like a big bloodless body, streets and boulevards are virtually uninhabited. Only two families have returned to our street. It is so hard, this silent contact between victors and vanquished!

10 July

Neighbours come back one after the other. But why are the Pichot so slow appearing? What if the Germans commandeered their flat, which is just above ours?

Life resumes little by little, but differently; we are all recovering.

1941

16 years old

August

Ukraine, long and undulating, immensely rolling in the wind, will you hold onto your sons in the shifting folds of your wheat?

It is said that the Germans have invaded you and half-stabbed you. We, who have already suffered the insult of their tanks and the insult of their planes, we fear for you!

A year ago, oblivious, improvident and over-confident people of France, we too succumbed. But how can you stand up to the cold organisation of such a rapacious and calculating country? And now, what do we have left other than hope?

"'What surprises me,' says God, 'is the hope, and I find it amazing. This little hope, seemingly so ordinary, this child hope, immortal.'"

Joseph Baume read us this long poem by Péguy, at the last meeting of the scout patrol.

Yes, "hope belongs to the French". So let's hope! We place our trust in you, Russian soldiers!

We have pinned a large map of Europe to the kitchen wall. Thanks to this, we follow the operations taking place on the Eastern Front. Kiev, Odessa, Kharkov will become synonyms of resistance and hope.

I caught my parents talking about the holiday I had missed. Holiday: that is a word which unfortunately should be used in the past tense.

When I think of previous years, I retain the luminous memory of seashores, now inaccessible, and wanting to dive into the waves.

When will I see my dear Vendée again, the region which had such an influence on my first 12 years?

On one of these holidays, the summer camp bunch had invaded "Ker Morvan". We had been travelling all day and had just left the slow, bucolic train. I did not mind it being slow; on the contrary, this was why I loved it. It was doing its best! It ran mostly alongside the main road, and we sometimes entered a hopeless race – for the coal was too poor – with cars as jolly as we were!

Contrary to what the leader thought, we were not tired and were dying to go down to the sea, immediately. It was less than 2km away, just at the end of the pine forest. "Tomorrow, children, tomorrow."

Well, he had to give in!

The sea, oh, to see the sea for the first time.

The night seemed long, long, and the breakfast endless. Finally, the priest gave a starting signal. It was a race through the dunes, with our feet insensitive to the sting of thistles; then breathless, with our eyes flooded with light, we received a shock! I remained speechless. Richness, power and eternity struck me all at once, whilst the calm of this immense beach bordered with pine trees, without a boat, without a house, flowed into me. I was becoming sand and water, just sand and water.

When I think that there are people who discover the sea stupidly, at the end of a road. No, it must be discovered by surprise, like an animal, like a wild child.

We did go to the beach twice a day, surrendering to the double bite of the wind and the warm sand. While awaiting the moment when we would be allowed to go for a swim, the priest, to cool our impatience, engaged in his favorite pastime: radiesthesia. It was purely amazing, what he could guess, letting his watch swing slowly on the end of its long gold chain.

"Hubert, how old are you? Don't answer. I shall work it out. Let's see: one, two, three … eleven. Weren't you born on the 11th? Yes Father! One … two … three. It's March. Yes, Father! Now for the year. First, the tens. One, two, say twenty … One, two, three … four … five. 1925! Yes." It was astonishing.

"Your turn, Jean." And the watch moved again, slow, heavy, obedient, and mysterious. I had sent a long letter to my parents that same evening to tell them about these wonders and I added: "Today, Sunday, we went to mass. There were many beautiful ceremonies, but the cantor screamed like a donkey. We ate a lot of good things at lunchtime, there are lots of cowpats …".[3]

This passage was my parents' joy. Often repeated, it is, I believe, forever engraved in my memory.

When I found out, the following year, from an older boy, that the priest knew our dates of birth perfectly well as he had all our individual files in the drawer of his desk, he went down several degrees in my esteem. But my love

---

[3]Cowpats were dried all summer in the fields, and were used during winter as fuel by the peasants.

for the ocean remains intact, with the need to run into it, which fills me with longing.

In Notre-Dame-de-Monts, one no longer hears the somewhat naive songs thrown to the wind by us children from the holiday camps: "Oh Notre Dame! Greet the children of the Nivernais with a smile." The only songs heard now are those of the Wehrmacht. Maybe their too famous: "*Der heller war zu wasser, Der batzen war zu wein. Heidi, heido, heida, has ...*", including the French version, a loose rendition: "*Allez à l'eau salauds, allez à l'eau salée, allez à l'eau salée salauds ...*" ("Go to the water, bastards, Go to the salty water, Go to the salty seawater, bastards ..."). How we loved those words!

Der Heller prefers water, but he doesn't seem in a hurry to cross the English Channel. Anyway, John Bull is ready for him.

1942

17 years old

July

Despite the "smiles" operation by the Germans, which only, incidentally, bares their teeth, the Scouts have been ordered to cease all activities. What an honour for us to be considered undesirable!

However, we continue to meet as in the past. It has been easy enough to change our label! The "Bayard Group" (the fearless knight, good choice for a name, is it not?) under the auspices of the Red Cross, visited prisoners and the elderly. We also performed in plays, generally for the benefit of associations helping prisoners of war.

Joseph, our leader, turned out to be a perfect director and *The Jealousy of le Barbouillé* was highly appreciated by the Nivernais audience. First performed in the suburbs, in Moiry, our company finally went on stage in Nevers, at the Rex under the executive presidency of His Eminence the Bishop.

In this play by Molière, which is not his most famous, I played the part of Angélique.

It was hell for me to put on a magnificent woman's costume, and to alter my voice, under the pretext that my features were a little less rough than those of the other boys in the group.

It is true that I was not the only one to suffer, since Bernard Rougeul played the character of Cathau, my servant, extremely well.

For a few days, we just had to suffer the jibes of our classmates and of the girls too, which we felt to be infinitely more serious!

We accepted all this cheerfully, in any case, thinking of the numerous parcels which were sent beyond the barbed wire, thanks to our new activities.

1943

18 years old

June

The Allied air forces have brutally bombed Le Creusot. To be sure of destroying the factories, part of the town has been wiped out. I have come into the ravaged city with a few friends. We try to make ourselves useful. We help the victims save the rest of their furniture, and load it onto carts or lorries and take it to relatives, or to a large centre assigned for this purpose.

We have arrived a few days after the bombing. The victims have just been buried. What a sombre atmosphere. But in conversation, not a single word of hatred against the great blind birds of death. This is war and it may soon be liberation for those who remain.

This morning I worked near the factories; five large chimneys have remained intact, extraordinarily, among the rubble, and are pointing at the sky like the fingers of a hand calling for help.

18 August

The "canoe trip" will no doubt remain recorded in the diaries of some Nivernais families, but above all, engraved in our memories. It is true that the period does not lend itself to such expeditions, since a curfew forces everyone to return home, like my great-grandmother's hens and chickens to the henhouse.

Eight going, four girls: Annie, Marguerite, another Marguerite and Marie-Louise, and four boys: Michel, Jean, René and Hubert in two canoes and a punt on the Loire. This wasn't really so unusual, but we had not been aware of the descending curve of the sun, and, above all, we had not foreseen that the return journey would be longer. The weather was beautiful, and no doubt we had better things to think about.

When we left Nevers, the sun was still low. I was alone in the punt, away from Marguerite, but no matter, for we would all soon gather on "Uncle's Island", which was the object of our expedition.

This is a delightful, small, sandy island on the Loire. A cabin, nestled in the middle of poplars and willows, is the only indication that it has already been discovered, and a small garden testifies that it is probably frequently visited by its happy owner, Annie and Michel's uncle.

He had been notified of our visit, and stood at the edge of the "greenery" to greet us. To stretch our legs, Michel suggested, as soon as we landed, that we should dance our favourite swing "Tiger Rag". I think that we must have scandalized "Uncle" somewhat, with our old wind-up gramophone, and our Charles Trenet records. Why did you bring, René, "Beguine to Bango"?

While we were pretending to get lost on the island, or were diving into the warm, soft water of the Loire, wonderful steaks and chips were sizzling in the pan, in the shade of the cabin. As the uncle was a good cook, he was permanently adopted.

The afternoon went quickly by, too quickly. It was time to think about getting back. "Uncle" was formal: we should go back through the canals; otherwise, he added: "with the current of the Loire, at what time will you be home, my poor children. And then, there is the curfew!"

Did you know that canals have forks, and that one can very well get lost in them? That was just what we did. When it became clear to us that we were not new "Joshuas", and that the sun would not stop its course for us, I was designated to go with my punt, which was faster than the canoes, to phone the parents, and possibly, to prepare a camp for the night.

I reached Guétin, the first small village on "my canal", just before the closure of the post office. I was in a swimsuit, and was leaving a trail of water behind me, formal proof of a recent fall in the bulrushes as I tied up on civilised land!

I could only find, in Nevers, on the other end of the line, a friend, Jean-Pierre Delery. I therefore asked him to warn all the parents that we would be unable to get back in time, before the curfew. He warned them all except René's mother, whose house he could not find. At midnight, braving the German Army's rounds, she went in a state of panic to the police station, to say that her son had left that very morning in a canoe on the treacherous turbulent and whirling Loire, in the company of three friends, and four young girls.

"So, your son cannot have drowned," she was told. He was in fact lost neither in body nor in soul, but was tucked up warm in the hay of a small barn. I had not been able to find any other shelter, but, in a way, what could be better than a small barn, with long, rough and fragrant hay! The next morning, at daylight, we had to set off home.

We got quite a reception! Michel's famous canoe, the *Ukulele*, was to be sold. Each of us was to go through the "family court". And all this because of the damned curfew.

Why are the Germans still in France? When shall we be able to live and play freely? We are only 18 years old: why this straitjacket?

When, at a later date, I am asked of this time: "What were you doing in the hot weather?" I'll know what to answer!

Late August

For a few days I have been at Trezillon, near Luzy, at cousin Glaude's house. I need not tell those who know the Morvan and its distinctive accent, that it is my cousin Glaude; nor do I need to tell my contemporaries that the "Rural Civic Service" has brought me here.

As soon as we are 18, we have to spend one month in the country during our summer holidays, to help with the work in the fields, and replace the numerous agricultural workers who are still detained as prisoners in Germany.

As cousin Glaude has not been mobilised, he has a beautifully kept farm, which allows me to have a pleasant holiday instead of killing myself at work. I go to the fields at a reasonable time. These are delicious hours. I like to hear Glaude losing his temper with his mare Polka, shouting "Hell's fire!" at her with his powerful voice, which is loud enough to make the neighbouring hills tremble!

I have always loved nature. There's something reassuring in its great stillness. Why am I so attracted to what is beautiful? I am at one with the hills, I belong to the clouds, I live with the flights of birds, and I melt at the thought that my grandparents have perhaps stood here, in this very place, quietly happy, gazing at "their" beautiful Mont Beuvray.

But there is always a "By God, will you get a move on!" to pull me from my reverie. Polka is very restive these days. And in the evening, when the work is completed, "Fine work, work well done," as Péguy said, I believe I hear a tired, but satisfied: "A good day's work, my boy!", while we head for home, thinking of the thick soup waiting on the range, which the fine white bread from Trezillon readily soaks up.

September

The Germans really do have some strange ideas! They want us to take turns every night at guarding the rail tracks, under the pretext that the Maquis sometimes blows them up.

With my notification in hand, I therefore turn up at each summoning – for how could I do otherwise? – at Nevers Station. The Germans control our entries, but not all our exits. They do not think ahead. Perhaps there are no dodgers in Germany?

So, why go and swell the number of guards, some of whom will most likely be selected for future firing squad targets in the event of sabotage?

I therefore go straight to a small backdoor, which always stays unlocked and unguarded, then I go back home to bed like a good boy. I must admit that without my uncle, who is responsible for rail equipment at Nevers Station, I might perhaps not have known about this lucky way out.

However, the next morning, I never fail to report to the station, to receive the modest allowance that these gentlemen allocate to the "good French" who help them so well in their fight against "terrorists". I have the feeling that the Charles Trenet or Django Reinhardt record which I will soon buy with this money will be particularly pleasing to my ears.

October

I have passed my baccalaureate. Phew!

Our happy student parade, though forbidden and broken up, then spontaneously reformed, ended up at the Majestic cinema. They were showing *The Adventures of Bécassine*, a silly film, whose title had nonetheless attracted a German officer of the *Kommandantur* (Commandant's Office). He was alone in the gallery, in a box, ready to enjoy the jokes of the Breton heroine. But we had decided otherwise.

"Oscar the skeleton", our biology teacher's inseparable friend who had happily preceded the parade hoisted at the top of a pole, began to dance in the light beam of the projector causing uproarious laughter in the cinema. The officer was becoming agitated, but he stood up, as if driven by a spring, when a firecracker exploded moments later next to his box. He left quickly, glaring at us with a look of rage!

We knew that the German police would intervene immediately. So we followed in the footsteps of "our officer", because we hoped to spend the night, after such a good day, in a comfortable bed rather than at German headquarters. Oscar himself must have quaked at the very idea. He was therefore escorted back to his dusty closet at the Institution Saint-Cyr, after a swift if not discreet crossing of the park. I then returned with André Gaudry through Boulevard Victor Hugo to 11 Rue Dupin, where my parents' smiles awaited me.

15 October

This week, D., one of our schoolmates, bought two large portraits of Pétain, and hung them on the wall, just above the teacher's rostrum. Indeed! Let him show his opinions in his own bedroom, if he wishes to, but not in our classroom!

There was a nice concert of protests. M. even threw a huge ball of paper dipped in black ink at one of the portraits.[4] Pétain supporters tried to beat M. up after class, but we intervened. Then they went to find the Head, and M. was expelled from Saint-Cyr. It's unbelievable! In some, I say some, "righteous" circles, the Marshal is God.

Will the portraits stay on the wall? If the Head attempts a showdown, we too will hang up portraits, but of resistance fighters of whom France can be proud.

The matter is not over; we have not said our last word.

We need to be very careful, for, as well as the Pétainists, there is an informer in our class, a fat snoop who is armed by the Germans. It is not the revolver with which he often threatens us that scares us, but his tongue, which is even more treacherous than his arm! A race of spies not even serving an ideal, but for whom self-interest and greed are the only motives. Difficult to understand.

---

[4]The following year, M. was arrested for resistance to the occupying army. My friend was shot at the age of 19, after having been tortured.

1944

19 years old

End of March

On 11 March, my birthday, I was invited to Claude V.'s house, some way from Nevers, by his parents. After supper, we had planned to go to the cinema to see *Evening Visitors* once again. I was really looking forward to it because I had thought it such a good film. Cinema becoming with poetry: how could one escape the spell of Prévert?

> … And you
> As seaweed gently caressed by the wind,
> In the sands of the bed you move as you dream.
> Demons and wonders …

Because he was born prematurely, my nephew, Jean-Claude, deprived me of this outing, but he also spared me a terrible shock! As he left the cinema, Claude's father was killed at point-blank range and nobody could or would intervene. Why would the Maquis attack this man? Was it even the Maquis? Or false maquisards, workers angry with their managing director?

Claude's father, as well as managing a large factory, had the unenviable task of being mayor of the small town. How could one run it without being in a subservient relationship with the Germans? Are capable men to avoid all responsibilities, should they refuse on the pretext that France is occupied? Who will do the job then? And how?

The most dramatic part is that Claude's father was a genuine resistant!

English airmen, whose planes were shot down in Burgundy, could testify that thanks to him, they were able to flee and return to their country. Claude told me he had dinner several times with pilots, waiting at his parents' house, for the right time to be taken back to freedom. They obviously couldn't shout it from the rooftops!

And then, what is worrying is that some groups of resistance fighters seem isolated, and quite unable to know why Mr "X" receives Germans at his house. Is it to inform them, or to better spy on them?

All the Maquis have good reasons to exist and fight and their members often behave as heroes. But also, sometimes, through lack of information or out of passion, they seem to act blindly. One cannot stand alone in judgement.

6 June

Despite the usual frequency jamming of the radio broadcast, we distinctly heard the announcement on the news: "The French speak to the French," which brings us every day, from London, a little hope.

Even when the news of the war and resistance are practically inaudible, we cling on to this unclear noise, as if to a friend's heartbeat. And then, there are these personal messages which are sometimes so funny. When we hear them, we are always under the impression that they are making fun of the Germans, and also that action against the invaders is getting organised. The noose is growing tighter all the time.

Tonight we are all gathered at the Pascaud's. We are on the first floor of the small villa, doors and windows double-locked. Emotion is at its peak because we are awaiting the most sensational news of the whole war: that of the D-Day Allied landing on the Normandy coast.

It started last night: we do not dare to believe it, but this moment, which we had hoped for and awaited for so long, has at long last arrived.

Despite its formal banning by the occupying enemy, I imagine millions of French people are listening attentively and ecstatically. The magic of radio is such that all we have to do is to turn a small black Bakelite knob to be united as brothers, in perfect communion.

Yes! They have landed! They have gained a foothold on the soil of France. We all leap up at the same moment, and pressed against the radio set, we listen to these strange words: Juno, Gold, Utah. Why did they not choose French names? Why "beach" instead of *plage*?

Papa and Monsieur Pascaud both speak at once, laughing, while the women, more curious, signal them to be quiet.

It must be hell at this moment, as bullets rain down.

They announce that bridgeheads have been established. They are talking of thousands of aeroplanes. This time, it is the real thing! It will not be a new Dieppe!

Monsieur Pascaud can no longer wait. He goes to the kitchen and returns with a bottle of bubbly. What a fantastic moment. A glass of light and sparkling wine soothes so many injuries!

Late June

Food supplies are becoming our great concern. The Germans are taking everything. We are reduced to our coupons and we are losing weight, every day a little more, slowly but surely. We do have vegetables. Compared to Parisians and city folk, you could say we have an abundance, but at some cost in terms of effort.

My father gets up every morning before sunrise to tend his gardens. One is adjacent to our home, the other at Banlay, at my friend Clément's house; he goes there on a bicycle and, of course, on this diet, he has long since lost any unnecessary fat.

Vegetables aside, it is famine. So we have to manage, take the train with two large suitcases and go to Luzy, knocking on the door of our cousin Glaude. The first part of the programme is easy, I could even say pleasant; my father feasts at the farm on a good *petit salé* (belly pork) stew: it is true that he will need all his strength! Then it's the return trip.

It is virtually impossible to leave Nevers Station with heavy suitcases which pull on your arms like police informers. These gentlemen from Economic Control sniff out good fat that comes from the countryside better than rats.

So my father has got into the habit of jumping off the train as it slows down, just before the bridge at Fourchambault. A short way away, wrapped in total darkness, I always await this moment anxiously. What if he were to fall? What if a hidden German shot him? What if he were arrested and taken to prison?

I am only reassured when I feel his stubbly, cold skin rubbing hard against my cheek. We go back carefully through the docks, then take the Rue Louis Vicat. I go in front as a scout, ready to whistle – as in *Cyrano de Bergerac* – a cheerful or a sad tune, depending on the encounters.

Finally home. The kitchen door is double-locked. We open the suitcases, and then appear big hunks of thick white bacon, butter as yellow as gold, and rashers of salt pork. What joy! In the eyes of the family, my father is as glorious as a Roman emperor, and I almost want to sing a hymn to the "God Bacon" on a single and comforting theme: "Bacon is wonderful ... How wonderful bacon is!"

July

In the night between Saturday and Sunday that followed 14 July, around 1 a.m., my parents were awoken with a start by the sirens. As they had got up "for nothing" a few nights earlier, they decided to stay in bed. Moments later, their room was lit up by worrying lights. Immediately, they got up and noticed that planes had dropped flares over the city.

Only the bombing could have woken me up. My mother therefore had to shake me hard, screaming: "Hubert, get up: balloons!"

"Balloons?" I understood, however, got up at once and immediately went out into the garden. The sky above our heads was lit up by flares that came swinging slowly down underneath their small parachutes.

I was starting to worry when I saw that we were right in the middle of the circle of fire drawn around the target, namely the station. Would the wind deflect the fire? I will never forget this sight, which was both impressive and terrifying. A strange atmosphere of war suddenly enveloped us in its huge, silver magician's cape. What would appear in the amazing tranquility of the night? Suddenly, fighter planes with striped wings – Canadians, we were later told – flew over the houses at low altitude, as if to shout at us: "Wake up and run, run: leave your houses!"

In a moment, perhaps, the bombers would be diving through this ring of light, scattering death. We hastily climbed into the covered trench, which we had dug in our garden the previous week. What a great idea we had, my father and I. The neighbours, who at the time had made fun of us, now ran to take up our places. The shelter was soon full. There were only women inside: a dazed neighbour, Madame Pichot, Francine, Maguy, my mother with her teeth chattering, and my sister. So the men lay down alongside in the garden. I chose to lie down on my back. It was no more dangerous and would allow me to watch.

Soon, the attack began at high altitude. One could make out the moving silver of bombs, which were diving towards the ground, as if they had been tracers.

I didn't think that their paths could be so curved. It looked as though they were going to skim our roof and fall into the garden; but they exploded further away, projecting wooden beams, stones, earth and furniture high into the sky: it all fell back to earth with a sound like a waterfall. This lasted for 30 minutes, which seemed like an eternity!

When the sky darkened, a plane came and dropped about twenty flares, as we might throw a handful of kindling on a fire that is dying..Their long bodies filled us with terror as they executed their phosphorescent dance.

On two occasions, the bombing got terribly close. We understood that the teacher-training school and the boys' high school were targeted because of their powerless but furious anti-aircraft guns.

In the trench, the women were reciting their prayers in toneless voices; they were much more persuasive than at Sunday mass.

Now we could hear, minute by minute, after the planes had departed and whilst the flares died, the explosions of delayed action bombs. We were to hear these explosions for days and days.

In the syncopated silence of the night, it all took on tremendous proportions. I was thinking of those who were buried under their houses or in their shelters, of those who were buried alive.

If we were to be struck, at least we would die in the open air. We had heard something falling in the garden. Was it a bomb? After some research, we found a heavy cornerstone, projected from Boulevard Victor Hugo! We heard later, at the end of that tragic night, that in an adjoining garden a neighbour had been killed by a similar stone. To be honest, I was more frightened after the bombing at the thought of pulling the dead out of the rubble, than during the bombing itself. I went to help nonetheless, at daybreak, after first going to Coulanges to fetch my friend Michel. Being two makes you feel braver.

Because of the time bombs exploding continually, the Mayor of Nevers opposed rescuers' operations in the main disaster area around the station.

"What good would it do," he said, "exposing living people to find dead ones?"

Michel learned however that there were teams of volunteers at the scene who were trying to reach survivors buried under their collapsed houses, but that nothing was planned to evacuate the wounded and transport the dead to the hospital morgue.

We quickly made up our minds. Michel returned to Coulanges to ask his father for the small Peugeot van used for deliveries in the city. Then, adorned with a Red Cross flag, we joined the rescue teams.

Rescuers hauled a few horribly mutilated bodies up to our van. Funny to think that I had never dared look at a corpse neatly laid out between two white sheets.

We were told of an old man, lying lifeless in the courtyard of a small house. It was the only house which had remained almost intact in the district of the 13th Regiment. Around Impasse Pierre Nepelle, it was almost impossible to recognise the original route of any one of three or four roads. Craters caused by bombs all overlapped; there was not a single piece of earth that was not turned over.

In the courtyard, we did indeed find the body of the old man. He seemed to be asleep: there was no trace of injury, no blood. We laid him on a shutter to take him to the van because we did not yet have stretchers. There were no coffins either, so the dead were piled directly into the back of the vehicle.

We then carried the corpse of a woman who had been thrown over the gutted roof of her small house by the explosion. With difficulty, her husband had pulled her back into their bedroom and hauled her up onto the bed.

He asked us if we could remove a ring she wore on her left hand: her son, a prisoner in Germany, had given it to her. Michel managed, after many attempts, to pull it off; but when he tried to slide the wedding ring off, he felt the finger was going to come off too. He gave up.

When we tried to take the old woman away, with the help of Marino and Jean Roy, who had joined us, we saw that she was virtually cut in half..We had to think up quite a few tricks before laying her down on a ladder to take her out.

Outside, rabbits that had escaped from their cages were running in all directions. Those we could recapture were handed over to the Disaster Relief Service.

When the van had been filled with corpses stacked any old how, off we went to the hospital. A dreadful smell was already emanating from these bodies. At the morgue, the disinfectant spread all over the tiles turned my stomach even more.

Upon our return, near the station, we looked in vain for the half-demolished house where we had collected our last victim. There was not a single piece of wall left standing: it should have been there! Twice, in the days that followed, we had the same luck, and started to believe we were protected by gods!

Little by little, relief got organised. Coffins were brought into the disaster area. One morning, while we were screwing the lid down on one of them, a bomb exploded, at the corner of the streets of the 13th Regiment barracks and La Rotonde, not far from us. We had taken our helmets off because of the scorching heat. At the first blast, I grabbed the one which was within reach, but it wasn't mine. Michel had to flatten himself hard against the coffin.

Flying stones were now falling all around us, in the midst of a storm of earth, when suddenly, shockingly, shiny red stars filled my eyes. For a fraction of a second, I lost consciousness.

After coming round, I raised my hand to the helmet. What a bruise! Thanks, Michel! What if you had been swifter than me? Below us, along the railway line, we heard a long moan. Getting up at once, we rushed off with stretchers, Michel on one side of the bridge and me on the other. There was indeed a man with a head wound, writhing in pain, on the ground. He was bleeding profusely. Marino and I were quickly carrying him to the emergency vehicle, when, by an extraordinary coincidence, Michel's father happened to be passing at the very same moment in search of our whereabouts. He did not see Michel beside me, but thought he recognised him on the stretcher. Injured? Dead? He rushed forwards like a man possessed. What a fright he had.

And this has been going on for over a week already.

In the evening, exhausted, we return to Coulanges, where I sleep in the room that Michel and Paul share. My parents, fearing a second bombing, leave every day after supper, cycling up to Saint-Martin-d'Heuille so that they can sleep safely.

These evenings are real moments of relaxation. At all costs we must forget these atrocious scenes, these human remains of the same family gathered in a single coffin, and all these sorrows and miseries.

Sitting in front of our bright blue dinner plates, we must no longer think about the pâté sandwich eaten with hands covered in blood whilst sitting on a coffin, and we must blank any thought of the little white dog with funny white spots on his nose and tail, who does not want to leave the hole where his house and his masters have probably disappeared. What loyalty to a happy family. There are so many men who would not have a clue how to behave like that small dog.

We are happy in Coulanges.

Fortunately, the house is large and welcoming. The G. and their old aunt are also staying there, for they have had to abandon their partially destroyed home. Madame de C. and her son are also among the "residents".

At night, the sirens often wake us up. During an alert, while we were preparing to flee, as we had been told, to the nearby countryside, Michel appeared, carrying "Auntie" in his arms as she was unable to find slippers or shoes. For a long time I will see in my mind's eye her long skinny legs flailing about. Was it delight or fear? We shall never know.

"Since you often go to the neighborhood of the 13th Regiment," she said one evening, "you should bring me my tweezers. I've left them on the edge of the sink in my room. You will easily see them."

"Yes, Auntie," for we called her Auntie, "we'll go tomorrow." How could we deny her this pleasure? It happened to be her saint's day. However, it was easier to find the tweezers in question in a good shop in Nevers, rather than in the clutter of beams and stones that had transformed her room. It was important that she should never know.

The next day, with the air of a spoiled and impatient little girl, she untied, at dessert, the first knot of the package that Annie had made, with her long and manicured fingers. I say the "first" knot, for there were a whole series of well-wrapped boxes, before she reached the famous tweezers that she recognised, by miracle, as hers.

Her surprise and joy were indescribable. We were her two heroes, who had come down from Mount Olympus. And we all thought: "Please God, let no one give the game away!"

Now that we're "perfectly" used to delayed-action bombs, we sometimes go the long way round by the Cathedral, before going to Coulanges in the evening. We watch the recovery of unexploded bombs.

The Gothic part of the Cathedral is very damaged, as well as two side doors. Fortunately, the whole Norman part has been saved. A machine-gun nest located in the large square tower – *Gott mit uns* (God with us), is that not engraved on German soldiers' belt buckles? – was supposed to protect the station. In fact, it ensured the destruction of the whole area.

We like to stop, so as to irritate the German soldiers, but above all so as to show solidarity with the civilian prisoners who are looking for unexploded bombs. The Germans, with their rifles in their hands, stay at a safe distance. It should be noted in passing that they removed only their own dead, but gave no help to the people of Nevers. "See what your American friends did," they seemed to say, "so just get on with it."

Yesterday we sat close to civilian prisoners and talked to them a little. They are volunteers and dig up bombs to make their sentences lighter. What a vile bargain. A bomb for fewer years in prison.

"It's hard to be behind walls," says the taller and thinner of the two, "I'd rather die here, straight away."

"Freedom or death," adds the smaller one, but without great enthusiasm; he was also the younger of the two. He must have let himself be talked into it by the older one, because he was waving a kind of long knitting needle around the bomb which had just appeared, with even less conviction.

Freedom or death! I imagined the great scales of justice with, in one of its two pans, a vast field of daisies, with a clear stream running through, and in the other a tiny skull from the hands of Amazonian Indians.

How many bombs will they have to unearth before they can run through the field of daisies? And what will their freedom be? Being reunited with a child who has been waiting too long? Or the smile of a woman? A smile, a simple smile is such a fine thing.

For now, they only had our presence and that of those cowardly Germans, who were signaling to us from a distance to clear off. Our last day in the bombed-out area was very nearly the Last Day of All, with capitals. After a bomb had exploded, we were looking for possible victims in the "Docks" district, close to the railway tracks. Michel was a few metres away from me, when we were lifted off the ground by the terrible explosion of yet another bomb. Shocked but not injured, I got up and immediately screamed "Michel! Michel!" No answer – I was unaware at this point that I had become deaf, completely deaf. Perhaps he was lying under this huge section of a collapsed wall. But there was no shouting, no call. A few minutes went by – it seemed a century – before I could make up my mind. Standing stock still, I thought: quick, I must run to the van to get help, he must be buried under this wall. He's dead! He's dead! When at last I could move, I bumped into Michel around the corner: he was running too, deaf like me, and shouting at the top of his voice: "Hubert, Hubert!" We fell into each other's arms, and so the terrible nightmare of the Nevers bombing ended for us in tears of joy.

The figures are dreadful, truly dreadful: 162 dead, several hundred injured and more than 2,000 homeless!

August

Sweltering and murderous July had ended. It was the turn of the German debacle to begin, 4 years after our defeat. We could guess by a thousand signs that the occupants were desperate. The Germans' nervousness was all the greater, and their reactions, like those of a hunted beast, were becoming more dangerous. Michel and I watched. The holidays were beginning to get us down and we knew why. Men were at war and we were tired of being spectators. We felt pins and needles in our arms and legs. At the age of 19, what could be more natural?

For some time we had been toying with the idea of joining a maquis. Yes, but which one? We had to choose carefully. Clément had just had a sad experience. He had only just enlisted when he had to flee and hide, in order to avoid having to "eliminate" a so-called collaborator. We sympathised with Clément: we did not want to kill a Frenchman in cold blood, even if he were guilty, to prove that we were men. We were therefore looking separately for a maquis which fulfilled the idea that we had at that point of what the Resistance was about. It was neither long nor difficult!

On 3 August, late in the morning, Michel joined me in the Rue Dupin. He had just received fairly clear information concerning a camp of maquisards hiding in the mountainous forests of the Morvan. Monsieur L., a friend of his father's, was supplying the maquisards with wine, and knew that, under the orders of English officers who had been parachuted in, they had but one goal: attacking the Germans at every opportunity. We still had to convince our parents, and then decide on a leaving date as soon as possible.

We settled on 8 August. To get to Luzy, we decided not to take the train. Frequent sabotages made it dangerous, and German identity checks were constant. Although we did not specifically look like maquisards, it was safer to take a different mode of transport. We chose a tandem, because there happened to be one at his parents' house in Coulanges.

I had only informed my father, knowing how easily my decision could be reversed if I had seen my mother crying. Indeed, I choked back my own tears when I kissed her on the last evening, after dinner.

My Scout bag was quickly prepared. We only had to wait for dawn and the end of the curfew. There are nights that count for a thousand nights, nights that will always be remembered, no matter what.

Outside, a long whistle. It was Michel with the tandem. Papa kissed me. He did not say a word. He knew better than me, no doubt, that words mean nothing sometimes, and that they cannot influence the unfolding of the days to come.

Nineteen years which lead to a silence? For him, it was the end of an era. For me, it was the dawn of another.

It was a cool, fresh dawn. Michel had promised his girlfriend Tote that we would ride under her balcony. Farewell, Tote! And now we were off, pedalling like mad.

Saint-Éloi, then Imphy: the weather was ideal. Decize: the sun was beginning to be warm. Fours: if only we could go for a swim.

In Fours, there was Jules B. "Let's go and see if Jules is around," suggested
Michel. He was actually there, on holiday with his parents. Jules was always
surrounded by girls, some of whom were beautiful. How do we know this?
Because we saw them in swimsuits! So that's how we left our route for a while,
glowing with our "future" glory as "future maquisards".

"We would never have guessed!" Elisabeth had said.

It was eventually very late when we arrived at Luzy at the L.'s house; they
were waiting for us somewhat anxiously. Obviously, we did not say a word
about our swimming. Without much conviction, I offered a simple explana-
tion: a flat tyre.

L. has good wine, his wife is welcoming, the children stuffed with
gruel. The image of this home is comforting, we feel safe. All the better,
since we may need to spend a few days in Luzy before setting off for Les
Fréchots.

On 10 August in the morning, at the station, the Maquis attacked a train with
a huge crane used for righting carriages after a derailment. The night before,
in Les Avenières, near Luzy, a coal train had been blown up. Was this a trap? In
any case, the area seems to have made a speciality of this kind of exercise. There
are, without doubt, sabotage technicians at work in the sector. That's what the
Wehrmacht claims, in any case.

Four carriages carrying soldiers and German railway workers accompanied
the crane. As soon as it had been stopped, the train was attacked by the
Maquis. An intense fog hampered the combatants. Because of it, German
soldiers were managing to escape. Half an hour later, the crane blew up
with a dreadful noise: the amount of explosive had been loosely calculated.
Meanwhile, the Maquis dressed the wounded and gathered prisoners before
returning to their camp.

"Rail traffic will be hard to restore," the inhabitants of Luzy murmured.

The German Army didn't take long to react. We were therefore not sur-
prised to see our friend L. arriving, out of breath.

"Quick, get ready, and let's get out of here," he said. "The Germans are
searching houses. We can expect retaliation." It was out of the question that
we should take our Scout bags, which were too obvious. It was also out of the
question that we should use the streets of the small town: escape through the
fields seemed the only way out.

After an hour's walk, we reached a remote castle, not far from silent woods.

"Nothing to fear here," says L. "The two sons are up there."

"Up there?"

"In the Maquis."

After a short pause, we set off in the direction of a farm set on the edge of the main road, 2km away. L., as a precaution, often left his car there. That is how we covered the road that leads to Chiddes with relative ease.

At Chiddes, we had a warm welcome at R.'s home and, since he is a wine merchant, we toasted the end of the German crane in style. Certainly, our attempts to reach the Maquis were placed under the beneficial sign of Bacchus.

R. handles certain connections with the Maquis. He gave us some information about the life that awaited us. He is a brave man, quietly courageous, with a combination of strength and lucidity. I wonder what my courage will be like. What will my fear be like?

All too soon, we had to leave our new friends, to go and spend the night at Larochemillay, last stop before the Maquis, which was now so close. The site is enchanting, and Mont Beuvray reassuring with its thick druidic forest; I have no doubt that my ancestors felt very safe there. The Germans would not be able to get into the Morvan forests, even with their tanks, the trees are so tight.

We concealed the car in the ruins of the old chateau and returned to the hotel to spend the night there. Sleep was eluding me. I wondered when we would next sleep in a bed. Aeroplanes flew low over the village.

"It must be a parachute drop," whispered L.

A parachute drop: I was entering a world unknown, which was both worrying and wonderful at the same time. I was becoming a link in the chain. I cannot allow it to break. Finally, I fell asleep, immersed in anxious excitement.

The next morning, we were suddenly awakened at daybreak by the hotel landlord.

"The Germans are in Millay; they have taken hostages, and now they are heading in our direction. You have only a few minutes to escape." The landlord's fear was so visible that we didn't even take time to dress properly before leaving our rooms. As we were still putting our shirts on in the street, whilst running in the direction of the old chateau, Michel suddenly remembered that he had left his watch on the bedside table. Going back and getting caught in the trap like rats was out of the question, especially so close to the goal.

We were now concealed by the thickly wooded park: it was wiser not to use the usual path, but rather to hug the large rocks that edged the property, crossing the road, and reaching Les Fréchots as quickly as possible through fields and forests.

We walked for a long time. At times, we found clusters of small aluminium shavings hanging in bushes and trees.

"Merry Christmas!" I said to Michel …

L. explained how they could scramble the German listening and tracking radio stations during airdrops, by throwing these out of the airplanes.

We were suddenly stopped by an imperative "Stop there!" from the under-growth. Soon, a man appeared on the path, with a rifle in his hand, and his finger on the trigger. Higher up in the thicket, we could make out shadows ready to move.

It was the first guard post, and we were finally meeting maquisards. The one who approached us was without doubt a local boy. He looked about 20 years old, and from the way he smiled at L., offering his hand, we knew that we would be able to carry on without further formalities. We were to be stopped twice more; a superb sub-machine gun shone in the bush occupied by the last post. The Maquis certainly seemed well guarded.

A quarter of an hour later, we entered the camp itself. I had a weird feeling of déjà vu, as I crossed the car park first of all. There was a considerable quantity of equipment, from motorcycles to big trucks, concealed in small clearings cut in the forest. What wonderful camouflage. German observation planes could fly at will over the forest, they would never discover the camp. But yes! I had seen this at the cinema! I was in a landscape of American gangsters. I clearly remembered the last films I had seen at the Palace and the Majestic, just before the debacle.

As we walked, still escorted by an FFI (French Forces of the Interior) man carrying a sub-machine gun and wearing on his ragged jumper a tricolour armband with the Cross of Lorraine, the old abandoned village of Les Fréchots finally came into sight. It was a village in ruins; its inhabitants had left it one by one, and there remained only two old people who planned to end their days there quietly, when captain "Louis" came to set up his maquis.

It was an extraordinary hive of activity, like an anthill disturbed in the middle of a nap by the unwitting kick of a summer walker. The main square was like that of a village on a fete day. I was not disorientated, for I felt as though I were meeting up with friends; better, brothers. Some stood near the guard post, others gathered around the HQ or the kitchens.

Here, we watched in amazement the latest German prisoners who had arrived almost at the same time as us. They were afraid; we were joyful. They had been disarmed; we were going to get weapons. We were not the same breed. They were the fallen sons; we were the expected children!

We were led to a lieutenant. We had to wait. He had a lot of work, and seemed in little hurry to enlist us.

Without a word, we went on to look at the surroundings: men and land-scape. We were finally sent to Dr B. for a medical examination. "Are you well?" "No recent illness?" "Have you ever camped?" Before we could articulate the beginning of an answer, we were already acknowledged good for service. We must have seemed healthy enough.

We went from the doctor to the lieutenant. First, we had to surrender any papers which might compromise our family in case we were killed, or fell into the hands of the Germans. Then, without any ceremony, he renamed us. Michel would now answer to the name of "Speedboat" and as for me, as the "boats" series was now complete, I was called, after some laborious research, "Will" (as in mental power). It was better than "Candour" or "Delight".

"It's actually a very beautiful name!" added the lieutenant.

The characters were now in place; how would the play unfold?

We were once again let loose in the vast camp, where we felt embarrassed in the middle of groups of older boys, like newly arrived students on the first evening back at school. We were a little afraid of looking too young, too weak in the eyes of the men whom we met, and then our clothes still smelled of the city.

We walked around the old village for a long time. As we went past a small house which was half in ruins, we saw British and French flags that fluttered, intertwined, over the front door. Two armed sentries stood in front of it. Out of curiosity, we went closer.

"You can go in," said one of the maquisards.

Inside, an astonishing sight awaited us. Two dead men had been laid out on stretchers: they were horribly mutilated, horrible to look at; what torture had they endured? Their skin was hanging in strips, their eyes were gouged. We stood there, shoulder to shoulder, absolutely petrified, for a long time.

By coincidence, as we left the cottage, we bumped into the lieutenant who had enrolled us.

"They were taken prisoner yesterday," he explained, "as they tried to prevent the Germans from setting fire to a farm, then they were tortured before being killed and abandoned on the spot. They want to give us a warning. This is actually what you could expect tomorrow, if you fell into their hands."

"Yes, Lieutenant."

That is all we found to answer, but deep down, we could clearly see the road ahead now.

Lunch time came. All previously established groups gathered around their "containers". But now, stew had replaced the bullets in them. Would we be left on our own, Michel and I?

Near the kitchen, a group of boys who had no bowls soon formed. The introductions were quick: there were three Scouts. We therefore found ourselves amongst friends.

We needed a container for our potatoes and the meat that cooks served up with big ladles. We should follow the example of the older men. A container which had probably been parachuted in the night before, because it was still full of grease, did the trick very well. "Ammunition grease is not bad with potatoes!", they told us sarcastically.

We had neither plate nor fork, so we ate with our fingers. What a fantastic feast! At the end of the meal, we swore that we would never separate.

Now we were twelve, and we even had a sergeant at our head. As a former escaped prisoner, he would soon settle some accounts with these German gentlemen, he said. We felt a certain admiration, barely tinged with impatience.

He immediately connected with HQ, to have his group ratified. He wanted to act fast. However, he had to wait all evening. Finally, a lieutenant reviewed us with a detached look, shortly before sunset. We left immediately with our rearguard, to the campsite that had been assigned to us.

It was a simple clearing bordered by birch trees, where ferns and moss grew abundantly as in so many of our woods. The Révol Group was to build a shelter there with two parachutes. It was beautiful, our conical tent, with its lined roof of green and white silk. Not far away, in the thick woods, opened other multicoloured creations. I gazed intently at this curious but magnificent settlement.

Armed men now passed by in noisy groups. They were off to the muster. That evening, we were excused.

"You must try and look good and march in correctly," "Révol" said to us the next day before leaving for the morning muster.

The night had been good and our ablutions more than brief. We were to meet at 8 o'clock, on the plateau, to receive instructions.

The four companies were already standing to attention in a perfect square. We were late, and we stood out. We were a laughing stock.

"Needle: march!" shouted Révol. He realised how bad our marching was, and wanted to apologise to the others.

We finally stood sheepishly in a corner.

"Companies: attention!"

The staff arrived. It consisted of two English officers – Captain "Louis" and Captain "Baptist" – and three French lieutenants.[5]

"At ease!" ordered Captain Louis.

Immediately, he began to give his orders. We were not forgotten. He put us on "spud bashing" for four companies.

Two days after our arrival, I was called to the HQ. We were finishing lunch. What did they want from me?

The door had barely closed, when I stood to attention in a pose that I hoped was impeccable. All the officers were gathered around a long table. At the centre was Captain Louis, and before him, a bottle of red-collared champagne. Surely, I was not invited to celebrate an unknown victory with them.

"Your name is 'Will'?" asked the captain.

"Yes, Captain."

---

[5]At the time, we thought that "Louis" was English.

Paul Sarrette, alias Captain Louis, Commander of the maquis, in his field command post.

"I have been told you do not look much like a maquisard ... it's true, your clothes have not yet suffered ... and neither have you! Here is a message that you will take to the post office. Give it to the postmistress when she is alone; she will probably give you another message in exchange. In no case should these messages fall into the hands of the Germans. You are on holiday in the Morvan, and you are out on a bike ride. Do you have family in the area?"

"Yes, Captain."

"Be quick, and good luck!"

"Thank you, Captain."

It was only after closing the door on a disastrous half-turn that I began to realise.

The day was beautiful, a real summer's day, and the bike was running well. I was not worried, because I didn't look like a maquisard. But I couldn't help wondering.

Were the Germans still patrolling around Larochemillay? What would I do if I met them? Any attempt to get rid of the small envelope would certainly be noticed. But why bother thinking of all this?

The Morvan is so green, even in high summer. It is an eternal spring of life. How can so many flowers grow on its arid granite, and so many springs flow?

I maybe didn't look like a maquisard, but I was carrying a message. What if I were searched? I know what comes next. Torture first, to try and extort as much information as possible on the Maquis. Then, the execution post.

I would have liked to turn into an insect and slowly climb up the stem of a harebell, or a water drop, to play on the side of a trout. I was only "Will" and had only my lucky star to believe in!

It was indeed very lucky, and with a bright smile, I handed the second message to Captain Louis in the middle of the afternoon. He was alone in his office. On his table, a field telephone and a small vase full of wildflowers stood next to Ordnance Survey maps and a packet of English cigarettes.

As he spoke to me, I noticed this time that he was speaking without any trace of an accent. It was good, for an Englishman, and I also noticed that even with his moustache, he no more looked like a "gang leader" than I did a maquisard. It was my revenge!

For a few days, the Révol Group got all the chores. We were asked to build board huts, peel mountains of potatoes and cut ferns.

Over the hours, we get to know each other better. They are darned nice, those in our group.

Révol, the sergeant, is a builder in Millay. "Cruiser", the corporal, is a gardener in a large house. He has left two small children to join the Maquis; it is admirable to risk one's life, when one has children, isn't it?

"Lace" has just left "Central" University, and his brother "Rosario" is trying for "Colonial" University.

"Jim" is an engineer with Citroën. All the others come from surrounding areas. They are farmers' sons, mostly: "Cargo", "Torpi", "Cotton", "Silk", "Wool", and then, finally, Speedboat and Will, not to mention "Needle", a typical Parisian show-off, who never stops talking nonsense with a Spanish accent, and "Cloth", another Hubert, born in the Morvan. He is finishing his literary studies in Paris. He looks like a poet lost in a camp of rebels. When he comes down from his cloud, he has unexpected reactions. I sometimes have trouble imagining him with a sub-machine gun in his hands. In any case, I will avoid getting too close to him, if we have to fight together one day.

One morning, we had a dry run, that is to say an exercise with no weapons.

"So as to get you warmed up," said Révol. As he announced that there would be an airdrop the following night, we regained courage at the thought of being armed, at last, the next day.

It was so irritating, in the camp, to be so close to an arsenal that was constantly in use, and to be obliged to wander through it, with our arms dangling empty at our sides. If the maquis were attacked, what would we have to defend ourselves?. One must feel so much safer with a simple rifle or at least some grenades.

I therefore prayed to heaven before I fell asleep, with a very special prayer:

"Lord, I know that you don't like the war, and that, contrary to what they claim, you never help soldiers – I mean, generals – to win or to lose battles. But please, send me a gun!"

Philippe Renard alias Courdoue. This 18-year-old friend belonged to a nearby group – the Révol Group. He is in combat gear. In addition to his British rifle with ammunition on the chest, note Mills grenades, a canteen and a first-aid kit pinned to his belt. The helmet was not part of the equipment of the maquisards, who fought bare-headed. Philippe had joined the Maquis with the helmet of a relative who had fought during the First World War.

"Lord, I do not know who gave you the good idea of trumpets in Jericho, or suggested you should send Jeanne to fight the English, but if tonight anyone asks you for a sub-machine gun for me, hear their prayer ..."

"Please, send me a sub-machine gun!"

"Lord, you who probe kidneys and hearts, you know better than me that all men are not necessarily good, but you also know that in one camp, there are necessarily more bastards than in the other."

"So please, do allow the planes to reach us."

He allowed it, as we found out.

On our way to muster, we saw numerous containers lined up on the fresh grass of the plateau. Carts had brought them from the field where they had been airdropped. What joy!

By mid-morning, while I lurked in the vicinity of the kitchen, where a few days beforehand I had found a cousin giving out steaks, Glaude's son to be exact, Lace rushed up.

"Hey, quick, get to HQ. They're giving us weapons!"

So much for the steak. I didn't have to be told twice.

A short time later, the entire group was gathered together round Captain Louis, who opened a first container filled with British guns. We took six. Then we were given six sub-machine guns, dismantled in their small hessian bags. Finally, a beautiful machine gun all covered in grease was given to us.

There followed the distribution of ammunition: canvas pouches with five bullet clips for rifles, clips for sub-machine guns and machine guns. Finally, boxes of bullets of all calibres and grenades, beautiful fruits of death, gridded and varnished.

When Lieutenant Baptist had logged all of the material received, we rushed to our tent like thieves with our spoils. Along the way, each had made his choice. But Révol had decided otherwise. He took out his little notebook, his well-sharpened pencil and declared solemnly: "Put everything in a corner and do not touch it. We are going to form the group. Each will have a clearly defined function. Jim, you're the strongest, and as you have already done some military training, you can take the machine gun. As a loader, you will have Speedboat, and as suppliers Needle, Cloth and Will."

I was with Michel and Jim; but also with the poet ... I'd better watch out!

The sergeant was already carrying on.

"The others, who are smaller, will be fusiliers: they will have sub-machine guns and two rifles."

That's it! I had no sub-machine gun!

Eventually, I did receive a beautiful rifle with two cartridge belts of fifty bullets, and a reserve of 100 bullets. After all, a rifle is more accurate.

Immediately, with respect, with joy, and boundless enthusiasm, we began to remove the grease, and polish our weapons. I believe that on that particular evening, we could have been asked to do anything; and I also believe that, like kids with a new toy, we would have slept with our weapons beside us, if Révol had not asked us to leave them at the entrance of the tent.

Do you remember, Needle, how you didn't want to give up your "Sweetheart"?

We fell asleep very late.

Then a new life began. We had just a few days to master our weapons perfectly.

Soon, machine guns, rifles and grenades held no secrets for us. We knew how to dismantle and reassemble them with our eyes closed. At the shooting

A rapid action group of the 2nd Company. They could be easily and quickly trucked to a combat zone. Notice their Mills grenades – often 5 or 6 grenades per man. The famous Sten sub-machine guns completed their equipment. All resistance fighters, myself first and foremost, would have loved to own a Sten.

range, we were hitting an extraordinary number of bullseyes on the targets; but, facing the Germans, will we be dexterous enough? When will we know the answer?

22 August

"Good news, friends, tonight we are mounting guard!" Lace said, as he returned from HQ. He was answered with shouts of joy.

Is there a single army in the world, where one could hear soldiers showing such enthusiasm? It is true that we did not know what "mounting guard" meant!

We were above all proud to march in front of the other maquisards, with our brand new equipment. We almost looked like we were ready for combat, with our rifles firmly fixed on our shoulders, our thumbs on the straps, the two cartridge belts crossing on our chests and three grenades on our belts. I was the king when, at dusk, we paraded on the plateau. We needed much less than that to feel like men.

"Section: halt!"

The group halted impeccably in front of the guard post, a dilapidated old house. Other groups were arriving, apparently newly armed sections. We wondered if this was the beginning of the 5th Company.

Those handing over the guard stood in front of us. A lieutenant reviewed us briefly. "At ease! Dismissed!"

As soon as they had left, we all rushed inside the post to reserve a place in the straw, as night was falling.

I was a little disappointed on consulting the duty roster. Lace, Jim and Speedboat were on guard duty for 24 hours at Mont Touleur. Their orders were that in case of alert, they were to shoot three bursts of five bullets. I was sad. I would have so liked to be with Michel and Jim, but I was designated to guard the car park between midnight and 4 o'clock in the morning. Oh well, war is war!

"Goodbye, see you tomorrow Michel."

"Goodbye boys: good luck!"

Shortly before midnight, the sergeant taking over came and shook me.

"Come on, get up. You can't be late for your turn of duty."

I rubbed my eyes, took my rifle and jumped from my perch. Good, so much the better, I will not be alone. Shadowy figures were gathering at the corner of the building.

"Biscay?"

"Present."

"Torpi?"

"Present."

"Will?"

"Present."

The roll call continued, short and muffled. Where was I? In the middle of conspirators? What was I doing here at midnight, with a rifle?

"Forward, single file, follow me!" said the Sergeant.

The column got going. The car park was 500m from the post. This park had impressed me so much upon my arrival at the maquis … Needle, who was mounting guard there, greeted us with these simple words: "Four hours are so long!"

"Nothing to report?" asked the sergeant.

"Nothing."

"Give Will the orders."

"Write down the arrival times of cars and their numbers, check all cars leaving, and don't allow any to leave without a mission order signed by HQ."

"Understood."

The column disappeared again into the dark night. The moon shone gently; it dimly lit all the defunct equipment on the edge of forest … I remembered

Needle saying: "Four hours are so long!" How was I going to kill time? When I have counted the number of steps in each direction, and learned off by heart the numbers of all the cars, what will I do for heaven's sake?

The first hour went by slowly … Suddenly, I heard a noise on my left; it was too clear, too loud; someone was coming from the camp, so I shouted confidently: "Halt!"

"Captain Louis!"

I rectified my position. He passed me by without saying a word, his machine gun balanced on the edge of his shoulder, and his arms loaded with mines. He walked to his 11 Citroën car. He loved night-time excursions, and often went out alone.

I felt like telling him: "Good evening, Captain, it's me, Will. Give them a good run for their money."

But I had learned that one never speaks first to one's captain.

Silence enveloped me again. It was a quiet watch. Certainly, the Germans could not reach this point without having been reported by outposts, therefore, nothing to worry about! Why were we guarding the car park, then?

An owl flew noisily out of the branches, letting out a long screech, cold as the night. I felt shivers running down my spine. And it all began. I thought I heard steps which were intended to be cautious, then silence, a heavy silence. I stopped walking. No, these sounds were the fruit of my imagination. At the very moment when, reassured, I started walking again, I heard muffled snaps nearby. Someone was walking in the woods. I quickly lowered the rifle and loaded it. With one finger on the trigger and another on the safety catch, I waited. The noise was coming closer. I released the safety catch, and shouted: "Halt there!" Suddenly, a shadow leapt onto the path. Instinctively, I assumed a firing position, but found I was only aiming at a poor dog, who came to me with his nose in the air, as if he wanted to lick my hand. He was less afraid than me! He realised this, because he told me with his kind, hungry eyes: "This isn't much good! Although, I suppose, for a beginner … Haven't you got anything for me to eat?" His tail also spoke volumes.

We exchanged a few sentences, about something and nothing. I never knew that a dog could have so much to say. This one even had a certain class. He must have been a pedigree who had turned out badly. I asked him whether he wanted to die, throwing himself in front of a gun like that. It really was a suicide bid, and I couldn't help telling him, indeed ordering him, to avoid the Maquis in future, if he wished to spend a few more winters lying in front of the fireplace!

He left all too soon.

I had to wait a long time: a motorcyclist set off on a mission, a section returned from combat and then, at last, here was Cloth, my replacement, whom I welcomed with relief: "You know, it's a long time, four hours!"

I could not find, upon my return to the guard post, even the smallest space to lie down in the straw. So I wrapped myself in my blanket, and spent the end of a long night under the stars. For me, everything in nature, explained this "rejection" and, while falling asleep, I pondered:

– the ideal gas laws, each occupying all available space, as if he were alone;
– the reasoning of Archimedes, saying that any "body" receives an upward thrust;
– and the principles of Anaxagoras, wondering why the other maquis had not considered me a welcome comrade!

Yes, 2 months ago, I had other problems. But all memory of the Institution Saint-Cyr, my high school, was already fading and, in the autumn, I would be at university if the Germans were gone!

23 August

The 5th Company has just been created, at its head a young and friendly lieutenant from the Spahi Regiment. He is an industrialist from the North who now answers to the name of Lieutenant "Alle". He wants us to see action as soon as possible, which is also what we want.

How will the Révol Group behave? Fighting must be hard. Yet, the first companies are always willing to go into battle, to pull the pin out of a few grenades under the noses of the Germans. So, why not us?

There are rumours, this morning, amongst the groups, of sensational news. But is it true? Paris may have been liberated!

Paris liberated! Could we concentrate into two words any greater hope and joy, and wash away any greater humiliation?

Hatred cannot replace love. We felt so frustrated, because we couldn't love a Paris covered in German flags, a Paris where nothing could be accomplished without permission from the occupier.

Thus, every breeze was languid, tasteless, even though it had caressed the newly born leaves on the banks of the Seine River. Spring isn't spring, if the heart does not feel its share of warmth and joy. It remains a simple physical manifestation.

> By the rivers of Babylon we sat and wept
> when we remembered Zion.
> There on the poplars
> we hung our harps,
> for there our captors asked us for songs,
> our tormentors demanded songs of joy;
> they said, "Sing us one of the songs of Zion."
> (Psalm 137)

Paris was a prisoner, occupied, divided, ripped apart: it was our silenced pride, an offence committed every hour. It was arbitrary constraint, a thorn planted in our living flesh, torture, and too often, blood that flowed on Mont Valérien.

And Paris might be liberated! Those of the 1st Company had apparently picked up the announcement on their field radio. Full of impatience, we questioned Révol. "Well, Sergeant, what do they say at the NCO's mess?" "I can only tell you," replied Révol, with a knowing look, "that there will be a big muster late this afternoon."

Upon arriving, that evening, on the plateau, we saw a mast erected just in front of the infirmary. There must indeed be new developments.

When Captain Louis stood before the five companies, he seemed very moved.

"Tonight, we celebrate a great victory. Paris is free, it has been liberated by the FFI, the French Forces of the Interior, who have just joined forces with the troops of General Leclerc."

I could no longer hear Captain Louis. It was announced that the nightmare of occupied Paris was over, and soon the autumn would lovingly turn the leaves yellow on the plane trees at Notre-Dame, and for us alone.

What a beautiful *Te Deum*!

"Let us think of our dead," continued the Captain, "of those who cannot, today, share our joy."

I was actually thinking about forgetting. How could we forget these past 5 years? Would this ever be possible?

And, for the first time, the French flag flew over our camp. The Marseillaise broke out spontaneously. It was a hymn of possession, liberation, purification, which sprang from our throats, a hymn which was both as joyous as a drinking song, and as profound as a hymn.

Rough men, real tough nuts, were weeping like children!

27 August

It was on 26 August that we set out on our first expedition. What a joy it was, for us, when "Constantin", a new sergeant assigned to our group, announced: "In ten minutes, we must be ready for battle, with enough reserve ammunition."

Finally, we were going to "go", at last we would perhaps find ourselves face to face with the enemy.

There was no question of being afraid; perhaps a slight lurch of the stomach at the announcement of the big news, but the group was so united that it seemed impossible to fail.

At HQ, we met the Menorca Group and a lieutenant. The latter immediately asked: "Have you received your additional grenades?"

"Yes, Lieutenant; three per man." (We were indeed men!)

"Perfect; let's go down to the car park."

One by one, we reached the small path. I was over the moon, with my grenades neatly arranged around my belt, I felt ready for the attack. Everything seemed wonderful, and then I was so proud to be going to fight.

The lieutenant gathered us near a large, old, green bus. We were finally going to know what was expected of us.

"We are leaving for Cercy-la-Tour."

Great, I thought, my grandmother's town! I know all the side streets …

"At Cercy-la-Tour, we must seize some vital equipment from the German engineers' depot. The Révol Group will take the bus; the Menorca Group will follow in the lorry. We will take the main road at the very last moment: I have to tell you that this expedition is fairly dangerous because of the frequency of German convoys going back east. Let's hope that we will be lucky enough not to run into any. If we were to do so, we must fight bravely and fight to the end. Any attempt to escape would mean a death sentence! I am therefore counting on you and your discipline."

Constantin continued: "The two machine guns will be in position from the start: one in the bus next to the driver, the other on the roof rack. Jim, climb up there with Speedboat, Cloth and Will, and above all keep your eyes open. If we meet German vehicles, wait until you are 200m away before opening fire on the driver."

Using the small ladder on the back, we quickly climbed onto the roof rack, where in the olden days suitcases and bicycles belonging to peaceful travellers had been strapped.

"We will be like gods. Travelling with our noses to the wind in this bright sunshine won't be bad! And what a breathtaking view!" said Jim.

As we waited to leave, I was thinking of my grandmother. Shall I have just one minute to run up to her house? How I would love to! And, already, in my mind's eye, I was pushing the dining room door open … Why does she always keep this room so dark? The sun, ever curious, gets in anyway through the diagonal slats on the shutters. As a small child, I was fascinated by these rays of light in perpetual motion, a world where dust motes danced to the soporific sound of the old clock.

The few serious gentlemen of the family, whose presiding portraits greet me from their old-fashioned frames, have always been intriguing. No, it is not a gallery of paintings executed by anonymous brilliant artists from the 18th and 19th centuries, but more modestly, photographs, rather good ones, taken by my Great Uncle Anatole.

Grandmother's brother-in-law, having settled in a charming town in the Cher, Dun-sur-Auron, certainly owed his vocation to a certain artistic sense, but this was compromised by a great love of idleness.

He must have hesitated for a long time, and then one day, a sign, lovingly painted by his own hand, indicated that "Anatole Carré, photographer" was available to take good photographic portraits.

Great-Uncle Anatole represents for me the incarnation of the larger than life Tartarin de Tarascon: same heavy build, same goatee beard, same mask-like face. His slow and pronounced accent from the Berry region creeps up and assails you, without a single muscle of his imperturbable face moving!

Though he has abandoned the black veil of his enormous and mesmerising bellows camera, Great-Uncle Anatole has managed to remain a character.

He had his favourite "subjects", I should say his models: his father-in-law, his brother-in-law Terlaud, my mother whose beauty attracted him, and my sister always looking lost, hand in hand with her little cousin.

I must also have posed for him, at the age of 4, if I judge by a negative found later; but I was open-mouthed, an unacceptable defect at a time when photos were touched up by overlaying them, between the lips, with a straight line of black pencil, to make them look more serious. Photography came in the footsteps of the portrait painters, and was still a very dignified art.

As I had not yet had my tonsils or adenoids removed, I was ruthlessly turned away. Filling the carp-like oval of my mouth, actually perfectly shaped, even with a good soft lead pencil, was quite out of the question!

My great-grandfather, and the father-in-law of Great-Uncle Anatole, reigns in the middle of the main panel, facing the door. Because of a certain resemblance – he had a magnificent white beard – we called him Victor Hugo! Is this why he dabbled in poetry? It did not make him rich, though. Attached to his memory is a prodigious and dark story of wells and treasure that we were told in the evenings, but the modest appearance of his small home in Vornay proves that he had never found any gold coins.

A second portrait dominates the sideboard. The first thing you notice is a wide, polka dot bow tie, then an ironic mouth and two sharp, electric eyes; the whole effect, with a straw boater on top, whose ambitious ribbon wraps a fine Italian straw, is fairly surprising.

I always associated this picture of Terlaud, a little masterpiece of aggressiveness, with the juddering images of silent films, his eyes overflowing with mechanical notes struck by a piano drunk on custard pies!

Great-Uncle Terlaud, I beg your pardon, Terlaud – he was the only one in the family not to have a first name, and he had always refused, in a spirit of independence, no doubt, any concession to a genealogical classification – Terlaud, therefore, progressed pleasantly in life, full of colour and preceded by the prestige of an American experience.

Why had he tried his luck away from the old continent? Perhaps he did not know how to resist the virus of adventure brought in 1917 by the US troops. He left to put his long and skillful fingers at the service of the golden-haired ladies across the Atlantic. He must have succeeded, because our Figaro, once he had made his fortune, sailed back a few years later in order to enjoy his treasure in his homeland. Unfortunately, the boat was to sink. Goodbye to the heavy trunks, farewell to the projects. Alone on the rough sea, clinging to floating debris, he had heard, coming from a large and beautiful wicker cage, a resounding " Are you okay, Jacquot?" A ball of green and red feathers was shouting frantically the only words it knew as an SOS!

This is how Terlaud landed, without money, but with a beautiful parrot, on the shores of France.

As a hero straight out of an extraordinary tale, this great-uncle occupied many nights of my childhood. He accepted that his destiny was as blind as fortune and love, but he was always able to retain, as a prodigious antidote, the smile which he never lost through thick and thin.

On an order of the lieutenant we finally left Les Fréchots. The low branches of trees whipped our faces. It was THE great adventure. Jim began to sing "The girls of La Rochelle"; our voices soon blended with his. We were calm and happy. It was wonderful to be up there, and feel strong in a warm sun smiling down on us.

We travelled for an hour before reaching the main road. Just before the crossing, the lieutenant talked for a few moments with a motorcyclist who had information on the situation in Cercy-la-Tour.

We drove onto the main road. Now more than ever, we had to keep our eyes peeled. After roaring through the village, we arrived in front of the German engineering depot, on the road to Nevers. There was not a German soldier in sight, but mines were waiting for us there!

With infinite caution, the bus and the lorry entered the depot, whose gates were immediately closed.

Jim, Michel and I had to go and hide in the garden of an old abandoned house, about 100m away, and watch the road, with orders to shoot only if an enemy convoy stopped in front of the depot.

Everything went as in a drill, and soon, loaded up to the roof with mattresses, sheets, blankets and an imposing load of equipment doubtless earmarked for our field hospital, we left for Saint-Honoré-les-Bains, before returning to Les Fréchots.

And I had not seen grandmother!

In Saint-Honoré, a huge crowd of locals and Parisians on holiday gathered around us. Imagine, armed maquisards circulating freely! They brought us wine and cakes. We were gazed at, questioned, touched!

A stutterer, and this was not just emotion, took a few minutes to tell us:

"My good, good ... bo bo bo boys, it's rea ... rea ... really good what you are doing here for F ... F ... F ... F ... France!" Needle, who did not know where to hide to laugh without upsetting the good man, concluded a little later, imitating him:

"If I ha ... had to s ... s ... speak at this p ... p ... pace, I would nee ... nee ... need to get up at f ... f ... four every morning, th ... th ... thank you mother!"

After this short, but entertaining diversion, we climbed back on the upper deck, and like new Caesars, we set off in glory, promising to return soon.

Today, we repeated this expedition with the same success, but the lieutenant made us avoid Saint-Honoré on the way back. What a pity!

28 August

It was forbidden to leave the camp without orders. Some shaved heads reminded us of this unbreakable rule. But how can you resist the call of adventure, and above all, the lure of a good omelette with ham?

Not far from the camp, Michel and I knew where to find a small inn lost in the wilderness by taking a shortcut through the forest. We used to go there at night. As dangerous encounters were always a possibility – the Germans also loved nature! – we invariably took our weapons with us.

Putting our elbows on a small bistro table, and smelling the waxed cloth filled us with pleasure.

In front of her black range with its three cooking rings, an old grandmother, wearing a large apron of black cotton with discrete small blue flowers, was busy.

While the browned bacon was mixed with the well-beaten sizzling eggs, the landlord put a small bottle of red wine on the table.

We needed nothing else to whet our appetites and, with our young wolves' teeth, the omelette was quickly eaten.

We always made the evening last by discussing the latest news heard on English radio. "Our business" was going well, now, and the Germans would quickly be pushed out of France.

Upon departure, as Michel picked his sub-machine gun up from the table, there was always this ritual dialogue:

"And how much do we owe you?"

"Ah! No, boys: it's for France!"

We wondered, ungrateful guests that we were, how much should be attributed to fear and how much to gratitude.

We called this somewhat infrequent entertainment: "the sub-machine gun omelette".

30 August

A German soldier. Blindfolded. A shout. A life that ends in a jolt. A body that collapses like a rag doll. An autumn he will not see. A mother who waits, who will always wait.

I think about all this, while I stand over him.

He knows that when the hole is deep enough, he will be told to stand in front of it.

A blindfold. A shout. A life that ends in a jolt. A body that collapses like a rag doll. An autumn he will not see. A mother who waits, who will always wait. This haunting and inhuman refrain has been obsessing me, for more than 2 hours, ever since I began standing over him at the foot of the big walnut tree, whose dense shade will soon fight with the lush grass over the task of concealing his body forever.

His pickaxe comes down slowly, without conviction. What is he thinking, digging the pit where his body will later fall?

A shovelful of earth, a few blows of the pickaxe, another shovelful … could we imagine a more tragic hourglass to measure what remains of a life?

Why have I been chosen to stand guard over him? I try to stop thinking. Is he thinking of the justice of men? Or of God's justice, so close?

To have been sentenced by court martial, he must be guilty; otherwise he would be with the other prisoners behind barbed wire.

We will never know what this man is guilty of; the judgement was delivered behind closed doors, but there is absolutely no possible doubt that this is not a soldier, but a criminal, who is digging his own grave; who is digging more and more slowly. I have not the slightest wish to intervene, nor to shout "*Schnell!*" because the word could not get through my tight throat. This is how I save a few minutes of his life; but does he care?

I do not want to catch his eye, I'm afraid of discovering too much; I won't, either, let my emotion show. A lieutenant approaches.

"That's enough," he says coldly. "It's deep enough."

Then he adds, turning to me:

"You can leave now."

With my rifle in my hand, I run away, to our tent, to find Michel, Needle, and the others, all the others. I want to stop imagining this soldier, standing, blindfolded, I can't bear to hear his last shout, nor think that a mother will wait, and that the autumn will come just for us, maybe. If we're not tortured, killed or, in our turn, shot. Shot like Jean Dollet and his father!

We have just learned such sad news, which has plunged Luzy into mourning. After the ambush on 18 August in La Goulette, the Germans, who had lost about 60 men in the fierce fighting against the Maquis, got information suggesting that telephone communications indicating the movements of their troops passed through Luzy town hall.

They marched on the town intending to burn it partially down. This was typical of them, as some villages in the Morvan can attest.

It was then that the mayor, Dr Dollet, intervened and offered himself up as hostage. By an unfortunate coincidence, his son, who had just joined him, was also arrested. Taken away and interrogated by the Germans, but in vain, they were to be shot on 26 August. Only injured, Jean Dollet made a last-ditch attempt to join his father, whose body was lying not far from him; he was then finished off by the Germans. He was the same age as most of our group: 19!

31 August

Because of the rain, the expected parachute drop has already been postponed two days running.

Cotton has, however, left for HQ, where despite everything, a message from London is expected. Meanwhile, quietly stretched out in the tent, we half-heartedly listen to "Eel's" stories, and the corporal's endless speeches.

After the 10 p.m. bulletin, Cotton comes running in.

"It's tonight, boys! It's just been announced on the radio: immediate muster in front of HQ!"

"Dress up warm," adds the sergeant simply. "We will be sure to wait on the plateau."

As it is only raining intermittently, I don't take my blanket; I prefer to save it to keep me warm when I return to the tent, where Michel, who is ill, remains on guard.

In groups of eight, we head towards the muster, equipped with long, strong poles, which we will use to transport the containers. There, we meet up with the other groups of the 5th Company.

After receiving instructions from our lieutenant, we climb to the vast field located at the top of the mountain, a few kilometres away from the camp. The moon provides dim light. The parachute drop is due to take place at midnight. Fortunately, the weather seems to improve.

As we enter the forest, the path becomes more narrow and slippery. Obscurity is now complete; I can barely make Jim out as he walks in front of me.

After a difficult walk, we finally reach the top, where we are spread all around the field. Constantin and I are sent into a newly harvested rye field, where we lie down on the wet sheaves.

On the plateau, three big wood fires, arranged in a triangle, are lit. The sky is dark blue, almost black. Wind raises and bends the long crimson flames leaping with sparks, and the men who are warming themselves on them form moving shadows which melt into the undulating grass, in a wild and unique vision.

It's chilly. I'm starting to get cold. Jim and Constantine have already gone to the fire. Quickly, I join them. The officers come too.

"Midnight," says Captain Louis. "They should not be far. How lucky: the wind has cleared the sky of clouds."

Soon, we hear a low hum. We quickly move away from the fires, which are loaded with wood and revived. An officer, with a powerful flashlight, sends the Morse message for the parachute drop. The Lancaster understands; the pilot responds by turning on his wing lights. Captain Louis, having identified himself, will receive his "parcels".

The aircraft prowls around the field, and its large black shadow, imprecise at first, grows with each circuit. It is very low, the roar of its engines deafens us. That's it! It has just released its containers, and immediately regains altitude. More than twenty parachutes open at the same time.

It is absolutely extraordinary, fascinating.

Most of us have never seen a parachute drop. While I observe every detail of the unreal descent of the containers, I think about these men, these British aviators so close to us, and who, only a few hours ago, were treading the soil of a free country. They came despite the flak and the Messerschmitts, to give us a bit of hope and also weapons with which to regain our freedom.

The long steel tubes, now very close to us, sway in the wind, and descend more quickly, it seems. They land on the opposite side of the plateau. We are apparently well positioned to avoid work and enjoy the best of the show. The multi-coloured parachutes seem, however, to fly just above our heads.

Two other aircraft arrive and drop their cargo even lower, probably because of the increase in the wind.

We must not move, orders are clear, before the arrival of a fourth "Lancaster". But it does not come! Has it been shot down? Did it turn back because of the weather, which has visibly deteriorated again?

Soon, there is a heavy rainstorm. As I have only a jacket on, I'm quickly soaked to the skin. As we head for the fire, which is almost out, a lieutenant asks us if we climbed this far just to get warm! And rather brusquely, he sends us to a cart where containers are being loaded.

The parachute drop, apparently low and precise, has in fact been greatly disturbed and dispersed in the wind. Some containers have even fallen into the nearby wood, but how can we get to them, with this darkness, and in this dreadful weather?

We must quickly fold the dripping parachutes, put them in their bags attached to the containers, and load everything, with four or six men, onto the carts. These have been driven by farmers to the plateau, which has now turned into a real swamp.

Horses wait impassive, indifferent to the rain, to the night and to the war. We swear as we slip and slide. It is true that some containers weigh nearly 200kg.

Once we have finished loading, we receive the order to return to the camp. The rain is still falling, increasingly heavily. The return is epic; the path has turned into a torrent, and the night is so dark that we cling to the bushes and slip in the mud despite the chain that we have formed to be able to move forward.

This blind walk lasts forever, until we come to a small lane which looks to us like an avenue. What a pleasant surface to walk on. Now that we are soaked and muddy, what's the point in swearing: a little more, a little less, one always gets used to a situation eventually. We may as well get on with it. So we do, and we launch into a drinking song:

> ... Fanchon although a good Christian
> Was christened with wine.
> A man of Burgundy was her godfather,
> And a Breton her godmother ...

When our quarters appear, we roar with laughter. It is after 4 o'clock. We quickly undress and snuggle down in our blankets, dreaming of new weapons, of precious ammunition, and of British cigarettes, to be smoked by officers!

I am also thinking that a tent can be comfortable, and freshly cut fern the best of mattresses.

1 September

We were awaiting the airdrop before we could leave Les Fréchots. It was completely out of the question to leave five companies grouped in one place. On the contrary, we needed to spread out, extend our field of action, and thus do a much better job.

The 1st Company went off towards Millay, and we went 10km away, to two farms near the small village of Chiddes. Yesterday we prepared the new quarters there in vast stables, with nice fresh straw.

We leave our woods and our green and white marabout tent with some sadness.

As soon as we have disembarked from the three trucks which have ferried us, our weapons and our luggage up to our new camp, and before we have even deposited our bags in the barn, Constantin announces that we must mount guard immediately, and insists that we should stay vigilant, given our new forward position.

I am sent with Rosario and Cloth to the top of a small wood where we set up our machine gun. The sergeant takes care of camouflage. He is very pleased with himself. I have noticed that sergeants often are. Is this typical of that rank? I don't talk to officers often enough to work out whether this is stereotypical behaviour!

I have already done a 24-hour guard with Jim and Michel. It's very pleasant when the weather is good, but unfortunately for us, the sky has been black since the parachute drop. We quickly build a small cabin for the night next to the machine gun, with foliage and four large blankets. We will try to sleep in turn.

I take the 3 to 6 o'clock shift in the morning, in pouring rain. Like the leaves of trees and dripping bushes, I am soaked. I definitely do not like rain.

Around noon, with the sun, comes a new British captain, who had parachuted from the first Lancaster the previous night, just before the containers. We did not realise then that a man had jumped.

He is about 25; he is the stereotypical robust and "unkillable" soldier, the kind of man who is never touched by fear, and whose very presence is naturally reassuring. He comes from Brittany via England. He has already fought with our maquis, and praises, in perfect French, the courage of our Breton friends.

I wait for evening with great impatience.

Tired by two almost sleepless nights, I am hoping to go to bed very early.

At midnight, an alert!

Four enemy cars have just been reported to HQ. Our group is designated to go on patrol, immediately, to Chiddes. We climb silently to the small church in two columns, where we hide for a long time; but we wait in vain.

"What idiot played this trick on us?" exclaims Rosario at last.

"Yes, let's go back down!" adds the sergeant.

An hour later, we are once again nice and warm in the straw.

2 September

From his earliest childhood, Michel had loved fishing. It is true that he had been well trained.

His cousin Pierre, a priest in a small parish in the Morvan, had tried to teach him the subtleties of line fishing and the pitfalls of Latin at the same time, during the summer holidays. But Michel had especially remembered how to locate and attract fish. Cousin Pierre was as familiar with trout streams and crayfish rivers as he was with the heart and purse of his parishioners. It was said that on Sundays he received the collection on a very large tray to better observe and comment on offerings! When Michel told me about their adventures, I relived in thought, with Father Chisholm, some scenes from *The*

Keys of the Kingdom. "The good Lord has created small fish, André ... and we are here to catch them."

When Michel asked me to go grenade fishing with him, I suddenly understood why I had so often found a smell of *Raboliot*, wild rabbit, in his descriptions of undergrowth and river banks ... he must have done some poaching with his cousin Pierre![6]

We couldn't go very far, because an alert was still possible, but we needed nevertheless to be far enough from the camp to avoid attracting attention.

A small pond hidden deep in the woods, about 1km away, seemed ideal. We got there quickly. Michel watched the water and the reeds at length.

"We need to throw one here," he said finally.

I was not invited to throw it, for he was the fisherman. It exploded projecting a jet of water on the surrounding foliage.

We stood up at once and waited impatiently for the surface of the water to settle, and for dead fish to rise, belly up. Our disappointment was great. It increased further after the second throw since only one small gudgeon was willing to sacrifice itself!.

Deep down, this poor result somewhat soothed our consciences. Our expedition did not stand up to scrutiny: the grenades came from very far away, and at a price. They were intended to kill men, not fish!

3 September – Sunday

This morning, it's icy cold. I have chilblains on my fingers when I shave.

We have permission to go at 11 o'clock, but unarmed, to the village church, where a mass will be celebrated. At Les Fréchots, we attended outdoor mass every Sunday. The Millay vicar, who joined the Resistance as a chaplain, conducted a very simple service on an altar built by our group with birch branches. The reverence of the men and the numerous takers of communion added an exceptional solemnity to these ceremonies.

Abbot B. is more than a Maquis chaplain, he is a true resistant. He had to hurriedly leave his parish to escape from the Germans who were preparing to arrest him, after denunciation by a man from Alsace who was in the Gestapo.

He had been warned by telephone of the arrival of two trucks of soldiers in Millay, and had fled just in time through a window at the back of the vicarage. From a bush, he had witnessed the invasion of the vicarage and the apoplectic anger of the tricked officer.

---

[6]*Raboliot* is a French novel, written by Maurice Genevoix, published in 1925. It evokes the life of a poacher from Sologne. Considered his greatest work, it won the Prix Goncourt in 1925. *Raboliot* means "wild rabbit" in French.

It was amazing he had not been bothered earlier, because since his arrival in the Morvan, he was in close contact with various Resistance groups, converting his house into a recruiting office, and his bedroom into a clandestine printing room.

How had he been able to carry on ringing the bells of his church to announce the services, and openly invite his young parishioners from the pulpit to join the Maquis rather than the German factories, without being arrested? It was nothing short of a miracle!

The young men of Millay were obliged to go to Germany, within the framework of *Service du travail obligatoire* (compulsory work in German factories). The priest had the bright idea of inviting them, with their families, to a celebration of the Blessed Sacrament. Sunday school children served as go-betweens, and delivered hastily printed invitations to the population.

The congregation was large and the eloquence of the parish priest impressive.

"It's not your mother country asking you to leave," he said, "but the occupier. By agreeing to go and work in Germany, you are helping the enemy to remain in France. Let those who think like me, come and find me in the rectory after the ceremony."

They all came!

According to their wishes, they were scattered in isolated farms, or joined the Maquis.

The next day, the mayor found himself alone, and could not therefore turn up at Luzy station, which was the gathering place for the town conscripts.

The young men of the surrounding villages, having been told, had imitated those of Millay. Eventually, on the departure platform, there were only the mayor of a neighbouring village and a few boys who had not been contacted to be seen.

The mayor installed them in third class and went, with fatal pride, to the first-class compartment where his position as mayor allowed him to sit. But at the time of departure, his young citizens, who had understood the situation perfectly, all got out on the other side of the train.

The train was expected in Nevers by civilian authorities, or collaborators, and military authorities, or Germans. Maybe there was a brass band, and flags, in any case, I like to imagine it. When the train stopped, the mayor, radiant, had to get out of his compartment quickly. He was, after all, the only one to have been able to convince and lead his small contingent to its destination.

Military music was now playing a lively tune on a relevant theme: "Life in Germany is a crazy dream, but crazy, but crazy!" and the mayor was already performing bows, shaking hands, and laying on compliments, until the moment when the oompahs were heard, on the deserted platform, only by a devastated mayor, anxious officials and angry Germans.

Morvan had not responded to the call.

While we are heading for Chiddes church, the call to arms suddenly pulls me from my reverie.

Quickly we return to the camp, to learn that two Germans have just been taken prisoner. Their small Simca car has not stood up to bursts of machine-gun fire. Officers are questioning them now, thinking that they might precede a convoy. We receive the order to go and take up position with our machine gun at the far side of Chiddes.

Well camouflaged, we wait for an hour in vain. Finally, two trucks going in the direction of Millay are reported. As the bridge is closed, they will have to change course and get through at a crossing 1km away, where we are heading at full speed to catch them.

Just out of the village, we hear the noise of an engine. We jump into the ditches. Jim quickly puts his machine gun in position.

I'm a little tense: in a few seconds, my first battle will start. I flick off the safety catch. My finger is on the trigger. Here comes the car; it's a small pickup truck; we must wait before firing. Constantin said that he would shoot first. Fortunately for the baker! Because the gorgeous, crispy, crown-shaped loaves he was bringing to our camp would have undoubtedly been earmarked for him. This at least is what Needle said, as he linked the shape of the wreaths we put on our graves with that of the prized bread supplies.

Quickly, we returned to the crossroads where we were sure to find the enemy. Unfortunately, the Germans had just been through.

Thus we had neither combat nor mass.

What a strange association: neither combat, nor mass; while walking, these two words continue to haunt me. They seem so opposed. And yet, they share another word: the word blood.

It should be known in Nevers that the maquisards attend mass! When I think of all the lies concerning maquisards, I am sure that they are spread by people who prefer this less dangerous approach to direct action. It allows them to have a clear conscience.

Our parents themselves had trembled when we announced our decision.

And yet, since we have joined the Maquis, not a single immoral action has ever been asked of us. Both officers and maquisards share the same objective: attacking the enemy, wherever he may be. We are the homeland army, and not the groups of bandits, murderers and thieves described a few months ago by a certain pro-German radio.

So there it is! Assassins attend mass, and they certainly don't do so to "show off"!

In September 1944, judgements begin, it is true, to be more qualified. There are fewer people duped, and detractors are thinking of other things now. Fear, which makes people ridiculous, is already rearing up in them, and puts a new mask on their faces. What a dreadful carnival!

In the evening, we learn that the 3rd Company was luckier than us. Near Larochemillay, a German convoy consisting of eight vehicles fell into a carefully planned ambush. The soldiers were quickly put out of action, or else they fled.

It was possible to recover two cars intact, approximately 2,000 litres of petrol and the most precious thing of all, tobacco, while the damaged trucks were destroyed on the spot.

As a ridiculous and stunned witness, a German prisoner does not know whether to thank heaven for still being alive or to despair for having fallen into the hands of maquisards.

Maybe we will have more luck tomorrow. We look forward to being really involved. For us, combat becomes a physical need in this highly charged atmosphere. We now wish for it with all our strength.

4 September

This morning, we dug two trenches arranged as a chicane on the road that leads to Saint-Honoré. Cars will have to slow down and may therefore be captured under fire from two machine guns.

Following yesterday's severe bombing on the main road N73, carried out by the Allied air forces at the request of Captain Louis, German convoys are travelling more readily on back roads, where it is our duty to give them a good reception.

Early in the afternoon, we leave for Millay on reconnaissance, without Michel, who has just left our group. He is now responsible for liaisons between companies, with a small motorcycle. He is delighted.

Using footpaths, we go around Millay, which we can observe from on high. Everything seems quiet. Lieutenants "Chin" and Constantin, however, go down in order to see more clearly. We hide in ditches in the meantime.

We hear two shots shortly after they have left. Have they been attacked? Soon, they are back. They were the ones shooting, at a German motorcyclist, but alas, too late. A large German column is in fact in the vicinity. We should pull back, fast, to take the information to HQ.

There are only fourteen of us and we may already be surrounded. Fortunately, we know the region better than they do, and we successfully catch up with our side without incident.

When we get to the camp, we learn that six aircraft will come tonight and parachute important equipment on a new field. Obviously, we will be part of the fun. I think with a smile about the first parachute drop I had awaited with such impatience, at Les Fréchots.

A strong wind has risen, and carries thick and dark clouds.

"There will be a fountain display tonight", said Rosario.

"Unfortunately, my Lords, we missed the last carriage to Versailles!"

Without turning around, I knew that this witticism was from Needle.

A few hours later, we learned from British radio's latest bulletin that the RAF had decided to cancel the air drop. Without regret, we returned to our billets. The day had been tiring: it was time to go and dream.

5 September

Louis is dead!

He was killed in a mortar explosion.

Lieutenant "Trystram" and five maquisards were also killed. All died instantly. This is impossible, we cannot, we do not want to believe it.

The officers could not hide the sad news from us for long; their demeanour and their sadness gave them away. Looking at their faces, we had imagined any number of possibilities, without realising that tragedy was so close.

Deprived of its leader, the camp suddenly lost its soul.

So I will not see him anymore leaving for combat, with his sub-machine gun on his shoulder. He always had the mischievous expression of someone ready to play a good trick on someone else.

I was thinking about the first words that he addressed to me: "Your name is 'Will'. I was told you do not look much like a maquisard. It's true!"

What would he have said to me if he had seen the holes in my shoes, and my worn out clothes?

I would so very much have liked, for his sake, to look like a real soldier. I could still see him, in Saint-Honoré, when he had reviewed us, after the combined march of the five city companies. We had all paraded before him and his officers, and he cried as he saluted us, so great was his emotion.

Seeing this strong young man so moved by the sight of the army which he had gathered and shaped patiently, over the months, from a handful of men from the Morvan, made a strange impression on me. We had travelled so far from this clandestine state, and from the anxious wait for the first containers full of weapons!

Now, looking at the progress we had made, it seems to me that I understand better why he had cried in front of his hundreds of maquisards: he might well be proud of them.

Above the farm, the sky has cleared; the clouds are gone, but they leave us with a sad sun, which fails to light up the grey slate roofs, which are still glistening from rain. Later, the same joyless sun was not able to warm our hearts either, and the day stretched out endlessly until the night guard duty.

Motionless at the top of the wood, I huddled over my grief in the dark night, and thought at length about Louis with sadness. It's a bit as if I had lost an older brother. I will miss him, we will miss him.

But "his" maquis still exists, and, with Baptist, we will continue the fight until the end, until victory. That is certain.

The Americans are approaching; we follow their progress impatiently on the radio, by intercepting messages reserved for the commandos. They cannot be beaten now. But it is up to us to do the impossible to speed up the progression of the bulk of their troops, to facilitate the advance of their spearhead, and, above all, to prevent the Germans from withdrawing to the Rhine in good order, with all their equipment.

How many human lives will we manage to save?

How many sons of Utah, or of Georgia, will be able to push open the door of their homes thanks to our action, in the near future?

Yes, I must fight for Louis and all these unknown brothers.

For each tank that does not make it, for every ammunition truck pitched into a ditch, how many soldiers will be saved?

7 September

This morning, we are burying Captain Louis.

A simple ceremony is taking place at Chiddes church. Our group does not pay tribute, but has been sent as protection to a crossroads from which one of the roads leads to the small church. I would have so loved to say a final farewell to him!

We are lying in a field, right up against the hedge to shelter us from the rain that falls softly. Nature seems to mourn with us.

We hide our two machine guns, and watch in silence. We have no wish to speak. Far away, we hear the bell toll: each slow muffled ring hammers our sorrow a little more deeply into our hearts.

In a few days, tomorrow perhaps, the first American Jeep will arrive, or de Lattre's soldiers.[7] What a fantastic encounter it would have been for Louis!

Around 5 p.m. we are relieved, but set off at once for the field hospital where we will have to stand guard over our wounded soldiers, again, tonight.

As we walk, I think about the "boys". Why had I thought of those from Utah and Georgia the other night, rather than those from Kentucky? Is it because of the Mormons of the Great Salt Lake, is it because of Atlanta and

---

[7]General Jean de Lattre de Tassigny.

Scarlett O'Hara's troubles with Rhett? Apart from an average essay for the second part of the baccalaureate, what idea do I have of the United States?

If we remove the Statue of Liberty, the proud city of Washington placed on the Potomac by a skilled architect, the buccaneers of Lafitte and the soldiers of Lafayette, there are still so many things to discover and learn! Of course, everyone has their own images, good or bad.

The one that the invaders wanted to impose on us comes to mind; it was, I think, just after the landing of the Allied troops in North Africa. On the walls of Nevers had flourished a particularly spectacular poster, showing a beautiful and flourishing Uncle Sam, in frock coat and top hat stamped in the colours of the Stars and Stripes banner, astride the back of a poor Frenchman, lying on a flag on the ground. But the poor Frenchman quickly found himself transformed, by our diligent care, into a "superb Adolf", with a swastika armband, a strand of hair plastered on his forehead, and a small, black, ridiculous moustache.

Generally speaking, we didn't leave many openings for this kind of initiative from the Germans. We must admit that they quickly understood, and did not try too hard. They do not like to look ridiculous and suffer from a certain complex of incomprehension. Let's acknowledge, in mitigation for these gentlemen, that it is not so very easy to occupy France!

This rain, which is still falling softly, slowly, and soaking us like an English drizzle, must seem very heavy to defeated soldiers.

Farewell to June 1940 and its cloudless sun for swastika tanks: it is all over!

The hospital where our wounded soldiers are treated has been installed in an old chateau, so close to the road that the protection we can provide without an advanced post seems quite illusory. I take my turn, from midnight until 4 o'clock in the morning, with Rosario. It's a bright and penetrating cold; I would appreciate a good coat. To warm ourselves up, we practise weapons' training. We really must be cold to get to this point!

I think, smiling, of the two maquisards on the same shift a few nights before, who had raised the alarm a bit too precipitously. Hearing a distant, but significant noise on the road, and judging that it was no doubt German tanks or at least towed heavy artillery, they had immediately telephoned HQ requesting reinforcements.

An entire company was alerted, and had finally closed the road for the sake of a combine harvester miserably drawn by four horses. It was actually, in the silence of the night, making a noise at least equal, to the ears of a vigilant sentry, to that of a Panzer division in perfect running order.

"I will propose you for a medal!" the lieutenant told them.

I could smile, but certainly not laugh, because I also remembered a certain little dog …

8 September

Today, we learned some details about the movements of the American troops. We also know that we will not have to wait long before coming into contact with the lead elements of the French forces.

Nine soldiers of the regular army have supposedly been killed in Luzy. Moroccan troops are reported near Étang-sur-Arroux. Autun is about to be attacked by the divisions of General de Lattre, as they come up from the south.

Our maquis is at a key point, at the meeting point of several armies. To spice things up a bit, we are told that tonight, a parachute drop will take place on open ground. We'll need to light fires on the plain, in the middle of this swarm of soldiers. What a nice St John festival! It may cost us dearly, if the Germans pass through the sector in any number.

The sections received instructions concerning their destinations immediately after supper. We are not going to the parachute drop, but to the bridge at La Noiselée between Chiddes and Millay, to watch the main road where the German Army flows almost continuously.

Significant forces are on the road between Autun, where the French Army is starting its attack, and Luzy. There are "Boche" over almost 20km, and as they are reluctant to go through Autun where the tanks of de Lattre are perhaps already in action, it is quite possible that they will use minor roads, to avoid a battle that they do not want.

How many are they? Several thousand no doubt, and now the time of the parachute drop is drawing near; it would be quite a show if the enemy arrived in the middle of the party.

So we set off to observe the Germans, and warn the C.P. (command post) in case their columns should veer off in the direction of Chiddes.

We arrive in the dark at a 100-year-old tree which has been felled across the road to stop cars and trucks. The surroundings seem quiet.

It has rained all day. The grass is soaked; we must lie on it nonetheless and try and sleep while we wait to mount guard in the branches of the old oak.

I would like to sleep and dream, dream of anyone, anything. Under the torture that I impose on my mind, strange visions emerge. I try to invent a spring and a China blue autumn, and to paint them on an old vase, on a fine and delicate vase, which may be too fragile.

I arrange my drawing laboriously, but the difficulties appear immediately. It is quite impossible! The more I remove the green, the yellow and the red with great brush strokes, the more they return and impose themselves in warm and dominant tones, spread onto each leaf, crush each flower. But I persist, judging this delicate exercise so much more advanced than the adding up of curly white sheep. Counting sheep really is within anyone's reach.

Soon I don't have enough blue and have to interrupt my work. All I have left is the dark night, the rain and the cold.

The faces of unhappy people take shape and dissolve now in front of my eyes: people who are hunted, tortured, afraid. How many are they, having to bear this same night, to feel every minute, every second, deeply, in their heavy, painful flesh, flesh which leaves you nailed here? No, this is unfortunately not a nightmare. Lucidly, I think about man suffering through the fault of man, about man who may become worse than a beast as soon as he is no longer alone.

No doubt he is right, Jean Verneret, a man I met fleetingly a few months ago, with his knapsack on his shoulder, living between woods and plain as a hermit.

And yet he has remained strangely linked with men; maybe it's impossible to separate from them totally, to move deeper into the forest?

At the beginning of the occupation, when bread became rare and was rationed, he had the idea of swapping a small plot of land, which he probably didn't care about much, for an unusual rent, quite simply, for bread. But he was soon assailed with doubt: what if arsenic was being slowly administered to him? Or else he thought that his freedom would not flourish if he remained so committed to this bread. He therefore asked regularly for money and food stamps from the amazed baker and took his custom to the other end of the village. So he was saved.

I am now thinking of a thousand things. I would like to accelerate my thoughts, to go numb, to become dizzy and finally to sleep. I mix confusedly all the cats who accompanied me through my childhood, the mandarin oranges I was given at Christmas, glowing embers on a wood fire and the running board of my father's car – why a running board? – with the joy of his return.

Because of my health, we then lived in the countryside, at Saint-Martin-d'Heuille, a vast old house between a large pond and a stream. Every Saturday, I would wait for my father near the pond, watching my friend Lejault pull rushes. I knew that he would arrive around noon, that he would slow down upon noticing me, and that I would then be able to jump on the wide running board of the old Renault to triumphantly cover the last 200m, hooting. My father must have waited for this moment with the same impatience, but I did not think of that. At the age of 7, one knows that one loves, but maybe one does not guess that one is loved!

My blanket has quickly sucked up all the moisture from the ditch. There are twelve of us shivering, with teeth chattering rhythmically. Lace has chosen to lie down directly on the tarmac; he claims that it is better there.

After an hour, having still not slept a wink, I see a heap of pebbles; reckoning that it is drier than my bed of grass, I lie down on it to try and find sleep.

Finally, I must have slept a little, or rather sunk into a state of numbness like a dormouse. It is true that the night is quiet, populated only by slight noises, whispered conversations and muffled footsteps. Sometimes, the distant voices of field guns are added in counterpoint. However, I do see with satisfaction that my turn on guard duty is approaching. I'll be able to relax a little.

The sergeant now precedes us in the small ditch leading to the oak, which stands out as a dark and precise outline on the sky as it slowly gets lighter.

Cloth and I replace Rosario and Needle on their giant perch. It seems the enemy will not come now. In any case, the parachute drop went off without any trouble, and the ammunition received from the sky, like manna in the desert, has certainly already been distributed.

Straining our eyes in the early half-light, we see a shadow creeping along the ditch. We can now clearly make out a man, a German, protected by his large camouflage poncho. There is no possible mistake; Allied troops do not have a raincoat of this kind.

We confer quickly. He is almost certainly a scout. We must take him prisoner at all costs. A shot would raise the alarm, and then who knows? It is better to be able to question him about the size of the forces behind him.

We slide bullets into the barrels of our rifles and wait. He is a dead duck! What if he resisted, though? It would be so easy to kill him from here, like when we practise. No, we must not! He is approaching, he is very close to the tree. He will definitely go around it by crossing the field. At the very moment when we are going to shout "Hands up!" we find that this German is, amazingly, one of us. It's Jim, who went on a reconnaissance mission to Millay during the night and who put on this old rag, which he found abandoned on the side of the road, to shelter from the rain.

In retrospect, we tremble at the thought of what could have happened. Yes, we could very well have killed our friend!

We look at each other silently. We say nothing to Jim, but what a clap on the back we give him. What infinite joy to see him alive and well, here in front of us! Good old Jim. Still, he should not have dressed up as a Boche!

With daylight, reinforcements arrive. The game is now won. We just had to cover the night. The motorised columns are certainly heading for Autun. Bon voyage, German gentlemen! You will be warmly welcomed, for de Lattre de Tassigny is waiting for you!

Once again, we joyfully return to the camp.

However, along the way, I wonder how it is possible to shoot, in cold blood, a man who walks towards you. I almost did! War is incredible, and ruthless. In order to kill another man, we cannot afford to think that there is a mother, maybe a wife and children. Otherwise, we would quite simply be animals. I was somewhat reassured that I had not thought of this when I raised my gun at the "enemy"!

9 September

Is there anything more delicious than a good hot breakfast when one has spent the night on various demanding tasks? Is there a more pleasant sensation than the friction of rough, dry straw against the body, when one has been lying in wet ditches or on heaps of sharp rocks?

Knowing how to appreciate is a deep source of joy.

The best philosophy lies in the relativity of things and feelings. But still, one does need to be aware of this. A phenomenon does not necessarily carry in itself a sufficient analytical value, whereas the reference to other facts is a certain value.

All these beautiful sentences came to mind, because I had developed roughly the same theme in my last philosophy assignment three months earlier. Today, I was doing the practicals!

Abbot P. quite liked my philosophy homework.

"For a mathematician," he said, "you could do worse!"

Personally, I liked the way he read pages of André Gide to us, his unexpected reactions, and his way of shocking, I mean his way of knocking us out of our usual intellectual rambles. Towards the end of the last term, he had declared:

"Look here, Verneret, this year, to shake up the philosophers a little, you can give the lecture about St Thomas Aquinas' doctrine."

And while the philosophers were actually blanching with envy, he stared at me with his small, wrinkled eyes.

Why me? I had raised my eyebrows a little, but I had had to accept; how could I do otherwise? If he had known that my so-called originality was due to a superficial glimpse of my philosophy books, he would certainly have hesitated.

For now, I must sleep, recover and, if possible, build up strength for the future, a future which may well be as tormented as a Buddha's belly.

Philosophy for philosophy's sake!

We suddenly awoke at lunch time. Indeed, how could we escape the rhythmic ring of hungry forks begging for their pittance?

On entering the farmyard, we discover three frightened Germans, captured by a nearby section. No, it is not possible: it is always the same ones who pinch the Boche.

Guard, ambushes, guard, ambushes again, and nothing, still nothing. Each second is long when you have your finger on the trigger. Not a single truck when we watch a road; we would even settle for just a small car!

They are young, very young. Their faces reflect a great weariness. They have the eyes of lost children. Maybe they are hungry. Might they be offered something to eat?

"Will, call Rosario and Needle! Have a quick lunch, and take the prisoners to Les Fréchots."

"Yes, Lieutenant."

At Les Fréchots, the central camp of prisoners has been set up well away from prying eyes and paths. We need a good hour's drive to get there.

Along the way, several trucks packed with maquisards pass us. They greet us with shouts as they pass, as though we were St Michael Triumphant, whereas we are simply "St Michael Conveyors". I really must take a German prisoner.

Our three soldiers are really astonished; they did not expect to meet so many Resistance fighters in the vicinity. As we approach the camp, they seem increasingly worried. They would certainly have preferred to fall into a trap set by the regular army, and wonder anxiously what their fate will be. Maybe torture? Death? Who knows: when you, yourself, practise torture, when you kill, you can expect anything.

I gaze into their eyes; they look like hunted beasts. I smile at the thought that between the six of us, we don't add up to 120 years and they are thinking that I am glad, because I can dispose of their lives.

The camp has changed a lot since I walked along this small path for the first time, winding under the trees. By dint of driving on it, trucks have dug deep ruts and the low branches, whipped again and again, have lost all their leaves.

We arrive at the old car park; it is pretty much empty since the disbanding of the companies. Now, on the plateau, we discover the prisoners' camp, surrounded by high barbed wire and flanked by machine guns at each corner.

There are a few hundred men, quietly parked here, piled up, weary of the paths of war and who are thinking or trying to think of what they were and what they are. It is good to see them reduced to impotence; a fair outcome. I remember, 4 years ago, the endless parade of our prisoners on the roads, and the young SS officer, standing in his convertible car, who lashed them with his whip as they passed. We have no whip, we'll not beat them, we are not barbarians ... but, in my heart, I rejoice as I see the master race, the race of "Lords", reduced to the role of docile sheep, kept in a park where the grass itself has disappeared, a yellow square cut out of the bright green of our woods and fields. Here, the Lorelei has become a simple rock at the edge of a dried up spring, and the singing of the daughters of the Rhine is now inaudible.

Is this an image of man destroyed by his own pride, or is it the justice of God?

10 September

The speed of the German forces' withdrawal has been astounding in recent days; the enemy has understood that he is not able to defend the South of France, and has withdrawn to his own borders in a movement verging on chaos.

We are therefore expecting the announcement of our own move.

At daybreak, there is a great commotion. We must be ready in half an hour, with weapons and baggage.

Gathered now in the courtyard of the hospitable big farm, we learn that we will leave Les Tillots and its courageous people once and for all. However, we take to the main road with the greatest joy. We know that it leads to Luzy.

Two kilometres away from the city, we find the other companies and make a triumphant entry welcomed by an enthusiastic population, who cheer us and cover us with flowers. Michel and I are invited for lunch and supper with L. A short time ago, we hid here. How far we have travelled! How sweet it is to think that the same enthusiasm prevails in thousands of towns and villages. Freedom is no longer just in our hearts, it is in our eyes, in the joy of our gestures, in the breath of our voices. We can dance, sing, shout, and it is so wonderful, to feel all this.

This afternoon, I visited my many friends and relatives living in Luzy. Hastening from one house to another, I noticed that my trousers had given up the ghost thanks to a protruding nail on a chair! I had long delayed this event by patching them, to the best of my abilities, with some chamois leather stolen from the German warehouse in Cercy-la-Tour.

Summoning my courage, I went into the first house on my path to ask for some thread and a needle. At other times, I would have been considered insolent. However, on this particular 10 September, after getting me to put on the grandfather's alpaca trousers for the time it took to repair mine, they offered me a large glass of liqueur and some cakes. It is true that today, all men are brothers! Every day should be a victory day. But wouldn't we get used to it too quickly?

Tonight we sleep on straw, for a change, but in schools, which have been requisitioned as dormitories. There are about forty of us in each room. Where is the fresh open air of the woods?

We just learn that the battle of Autun is now over and that troops of General de Lattre de Tassigny won a great victory and took a great number of prisoners!

11 September

The L. have adopted us. We will have all our meals at their house. They are so nice! We do not miss the camp's kitchen, with its endless potatoes in gravy, and its tough meat that has not been hung.

Very early, we leave by truck on the road to Autun, in search of the Boche. To move forwards, our lorry must avoid truck wrecks or burnt-out remains of cars, guns, tanks and other tracked vehicles. The ditches are filled with shells, ammunition of all kinds, rifles, gas masks.

This road to Autun is really the road of death, where tired, exhausted German soldiers have stretched out and are still stretching out in long columns. They drive, they flee rather, ahead of de Lattre de Tassigny's army, ahead of the Royal Air Force which sprays them with bullets and bombs, ahead of the maquisards finally, who attack them by surprise at any time.

It is always the same scenario that unfolds on these roads, alongside woods and their treacherous slopes. Small convoys are spotted, the first truck driver is killed by machine-gun crossfire, and the grenade and machine-gun carnage begins. Germans often don't have time to respond to the hail of bullets from automatic weapons; they are killed or taken prisoner before they can react. So many fights, some of which turn into real battles, when blocked trucks are only a vanguard.

We leave this sinister road to go and check a small wood and chateau near Magny. Farmers report that a German cavalry regiment stationed there last night, but they don't know whether they have left or not.

The sergeant asks for a volunteer to scout round the chateau, in order to observe the size of enemy forces. There is always a moment's silence. It may be very short, but it seems an eternity. I put my hand up, like I did at school.

"Me, Sergeant, maybe?"

I'd had enough of chasing Germans in vain; hopefully, this time, I should be more successful. I slide a bullet into the chamber of my gun and slip silently into the wood. I try and melt into the shadows as I walk next to a path which must, without doubt, lead indirectly to the chateau.

The wood is quiet. But if it is occupied, I'll be seen before I can see. Perhaps at this very moment, a German is quietly getting me in his sights; within 2 seconds, he will shoot; I can feel it … one second left … This feeling is so vivid that I leap aside to avoid the bullet. But it's silly. You wouldn't be afraid, would you, Will?

I must move forward and think about something else.

But how could you not think that you will get burned, if you run your finger through the flame of a candle? Is it enough to be brave? First of all, it doesn't mean anything, being brave! The courage of some is not the courage of others. Nothing is more subjective. There must be twenty kinds of courage:

- the courage of the soldier, who is afraid,
- the courage of the soldier, who is never afraid,
- the courage of the soldier who does not know he is in danger.

These three make three very different soldiers. However, what if they are all three dead? Well, all three will be buried, with the same honours. They will be given three medals, posthumously, of course!

Three men, three lives, three deaths and three medals: it all adds up!

No, not quite, not really.

Upon reflection, I would almost agree with Hector when he says: "As dead as you may be, there is among you the same proportion of brave men and cowards as among us, who survived, and you won't make me confuse the dead that I admire with the dead that I do not admire by means of a ceremony!"

And, what if the bravest man were in fact the most fearful?

I am pursuing my approach carefully, but with less anxiety.

About the soldier who does not know that he is in danger, I had understood the difference between "fear" and "ignorance of the facts" a few years ago.

It was a Maundy Thursday, I was 12 years old, and I was a choirboy at Saint-Étienne de Nevers. As every year during Holy Week, we would go, generally in groups of three, and bless the houses. We received in exchange a few coins, some eggs or even cakes and sweets.

My two companions were probably a little older or less naive than me, I no longer quite remember. The fact remains that they had carefully and secretly calculated that in blessing one house out of three in turn, I should inevitably end up in front of an establishment with a large lantern outside, that morality condemns, but that the world tolerates.

So we started down the Rue Aublanc.

Having arrived in front of the large building in question, I knocked on a beautiful upholstered door, before entering as innocently as you please. The light inside was gently subdued. A few notes of bright colour put me completely at ease, until the arrival of a lady of a certain age, who looked at me with some surprise. I was indeed wearing a red cassock, with a white, well-starched lace surplice, and I was holding my bucket of holy water in one hand, while the other was preparing to brandish the aspersorium.

"Madame, it is Holy Thursday, and I have come to bless the house!"

She replied with relief: "Well, go on, young man!"

With the usual ceremonial, I crossed the vast room in every direction, spraying it generously with holy water.

"This is for you," she said, when I had finished, dropping a big coin into my hand.

Back in the street, I found my two friends roaring with laughter. They cheerfully explained things to me. Their triumph was part of the game: my astonished gaze only increased their intense jubilation. Apparently, I had shown great bravery going in there!

Scarcity is sometimes synonymous with value. I may have had no courage, but I could now pride myself in having blessed such a house and taken some profit in hard cash from a lady who usually makes it.

I now approach the chateau; just a few hundred metres left before the edge of the wood. Surely a regiment makes a noise? I stop, listen at length: nothing. I gently continue my progress, and crouch down when I reach the edge of the woods. However much I strain to see, I can only make out straw scattered in the large courtyard, empty boxes and an old field kitchen that has given up the ghost. No doubt about it, they have moved on. I run back to my group. There will be no action today. Fate is against me: I am regularly denied opportunities for being "heroic"!

12 September

We have searched and criss-crossed a huge forest, without any result, other than that our calves appear to adapt very badly to this 30km zigzag through the undergrowth. I fall asleep on my diary, as I write.

13 September

Guard in Chigy, a few kilometres from Luzy. We are at an important crossroads, and must report any German convoys, so that they receive the welcome they deserve upon their arrival in the neighbourhood.

It is true that they are becoming less frequent, and we can only hope for latecomers.

Some nearby farmers, informed of our presence, bring us three big roasted chickens, with chips, around midday. For twelve of us, we can't complain, especially since, in the bottom of the baskets, we can see beautiful white cheeses, crème fraiche and pies. As the neighbouring meadow has spread its prettiest flowered tablecloth under the apple trees, and the sun is also playing its part, we feel cheerful.

After this delicious day of relaxation in the grass, we return to Luzy, leaving for those who are to replace us three chicken carcasses, and hope for renewed generosity for the evening meal!

17 September

Great event! After a week spent in endless running on roads, up hill and down dale, we are sent into the excited atmosphere of a spa town with all our weaponry, for a change of scene.

Dressed as we are as maquisards, ripped by thorns and brambles, dirty from dusty tracks, we are rushed into the joyful and smart welcome of Saint-Honoré-les-Bains.

The church has opened the heavy panels of its doors to our flag, escorted by soldiers choked by the honour.

The church is too small to welcome all of us, so outside, we, the pagan ones, have the impression of having accomplished "something" and we soak up the flattering looks given to those who have chosen the right side. We take on the superior countenance of those who have done well.

Now, at the end of the service, all the bells ring out to say to the population, along with Captain Baptist: "All these boys, your boys, are hungry: fresh air in the woods whets the appetite, so would you invite them for lunch?"

And it is a swift wave of friendship which sweeps over us. In just a few moments, I get five invitations. I accept the first invitation for the boy is friendly.

When we get close to a spacious villa, he disappears or changes by some prodigious metamorphosis into a beautiful blonde girl. The fairy that stands at her side, for she can only be a fairy, is to be called Aunt Juliette.

After welcoming me with some surprise, Aunt Juliette who perhaps finds me very young for a victor, brings us a drink that looks like an aperitif.

Her name is Michele, the young and amazing person who invited me. With a flickering of her eyelids similar to the pre-marital flight of a kind of butterfly to be found on the Cyclades islands, she toasts our victory. This does not fit with her. She is much too fragile. There are toasts that cannot be proposed when one is only 17, and has very pale blue eyes, and a trembling bust lost in the vast field of flowers of a light green blouse.

The aunt, meanwhile, says nothing.

Settled on the brown leather of a big armchair, with my weapons and ammunition at my feet, I think I hear, with a certain complacency, inhuman words buzzing in my ears.

"... For yours is the kingdom, and the power, and the glory ..." Why are the words inhuman? Would glory be a divine article? I agree about the power, but the glory? I imagine it better with the Deadly Sins, the eighth, perhaps, right next to pride.

The lunch is excellent and the aunt is mostly in the kitchen, busy preparing her sauces. I would have liked the aunt to be called Michele, leaving me alone with my Juliette, side by side at the table. Romeo can dream on!

Suddenly, whistles are heard. I hurriedly pick up rifle, cartridge belts and grenades, and hurry to the meeting point. Captain Baptist seems very angry. Several "Attention!" – "At ease!" are repeated and, at the confused noise which covers each command, I have to acknowledge that far more wine than water has been flowing in the town of Saint-Honoré-les-Bains.

Captain Baptist speaks. He gives us a heartfelt reprimand: "Certain characters have attempted to shave two women. They are in prison. It is not your role to deliver justice. To each their own job. You take care of the Germans, that's enough. Now, I must warn you that at the slightest breach of orders, this evening's dances and balls will be cancelled, and we will immediately return to Luzy, on foot. At ease! Dismissed."

It is loud and clear. For my part, I would rather go dancing than play with hairdresser's scissors but I also think that spirits overheated by the juice of the vine could very well indulge in actions for which we would all bear the consequences, whether we liked it or not. Eventually, however, all ended well.

We danced all night in many places. What an extraordinary atmosphere, especially at the officers' and non-commissioned officers' ball, which I managed to sneak into with Michele, while Aunt Juliette had long since been asleep. A pretty girl can be the best passport, it would seem!

I must have stepped on her toes a fair bit while dancing the tango. This is not, alas, my speciality.

"To the joyous sound of the balalaika, I was exhilarated with love and vodka."

Instead of vodka, it was champagne that flowed all night long, at the Hôtel du Guet.

At daybreak, with our legs a little weak, we got back in the trucks, sorry to leave the small town where we had already made so many good friends.

18 September

It wasn't Luzy that the trucks took our company to, but directly to Sémelay, where a surprise party similar to the one the evening before was waiting for us.

"You used to mount guard two nights in a row, so why would you not dance again tonight?" asked the sergeant, pretending to look gruff.

The people of Sémelay also intended to welcome us honourably. Had we not, after all, prevented their homes and their farms from burning?

I am appointed by our lieutenant to be part of the colour party. I deeply appreciate it.

During the minute's silence in front of the 1914–18 war memorial, I absent-mindedly read on the small stone memorial the names of those who fell to the enemy. I discover to my amazement, two Verneret: Claude Verneret, 10 December 1914; Jean Verneret, 13 November 1917. Two cousins, no doubt. I link their sacrifice to the joy I feel at being here today, in Sémelay, in their liberated Morvan.

We enter the church with the flag, and the five of us stand to attention in the choir.

For over an hour during the ceremony, I dare not make the slightest movement; I feel no weariness, however. Is this pride?

After the mass, a champagne reception and a magnificent banquet are served in the classrooms of the local school, then we have the ball, our swollen feet in shoes that had given up the ghost long ago, and finally, we return to the camp late at night.

Completely worn out, we lie down on the same straw as the prisoners, but we certainly find it much less rough. It is simply a matter of heart.

20 September

The prisoners, who have left Les Fréchots, are now installed in large sheds on the outskirts of Luzy. They wait patiently before being moved on, pleased to still be alive. We take the opportunity of swapping their boots for our ruined shoes. Obviously, they resist a little, but our arguments are persuasive. It is forbidden to trade anything and officers punish traders severely; but we deal anyway, in secret. It is difficult to prove that the boots were taken from a prisoner rather than from a dead soldier on the road to Autun.

Finally I have decided to abandon my own clodhoppers, which have had it, although operating in this warehouse is risky. I don't fancy having my head shaved. I will therefore ask for a guard duty on a cleaning shift.

22 September

Armed with a good sub-machine gun, sitting on a wall where I must have sat very often as a child, I now watch my five Germans, and thoroughly enjoy the spectacle of these soldiers "armed" with shovels and brooms, cleaning my hometown.

Opposite the church, they load a heap of rubbish. Later on, when we are in the quarry, I shall decide. It is quite possible that I shall begin my fitting with the little brown-haired chap who seems reluctant to get on with the job and has already challenged the butt of my gun. As he has fat buttocks, I can't have hurt him very badly.

Now that we are alone and far from Luzy, I'll finally be able to take action. As the countryside does not seem to inspire my little church mutineer more than the city, he is definitely the one that I invite to follow me along the rutted shady path bordering the quarry. As he has into the bargain a beautiful pair of flexible brown boots, I feel that my choice is doubly justified.

All irony has left his expression, which is suddenly alive with fear. The change was quick, but I was watching his eyes.

He anxiously walks ahead of me, turning his head at times, trying to guess my intentions. He knows that for want of law, I have all power over him. As in all the armies of the world, to justify myself, I will only have to say: "He tried to escape, so I had to shoot!"

"Move!"

I push him with my machine gun. When he feels the metal against his back, the trembling that shakes him tells me that fear is giving way to panic.

"*Schnell!*"

But the ordeal has gone on long enough, I'm not a torturer.

"Take off your boots!"

He obeys at once, almost happy, for he has understood. One does not ask someone who is about to be executed to take off his boots.

We are now face to face, in socks, as ridiculous as each other; and, since they have huge holes, I almost feel like laughing. War really isn't serious, sometimes!

But the boots are too large, far too large; I give them back to him, and furious, put my broken shoes back on.

Shall I be luckier with the second prisoner? He is old. He must be a soldier of the Territorial Reserve. What is he doing here, lost in France?

Sitting down, he pulls at the heel of a boot, with great difficulty, it would seem; in any case, without enthusiasm.

"Give, just one, to try it on."

Great! My foot is perfectly comfortable.

"Now, the other."

It is then that the drama breaks out: he starts to speak hurriedly in German, and his sentences, which are incomprehensible to me, are interspersed with tears. It is enough to stifle any ambition, to stop dead any spirit of conquest.

"If you …", and he makes me understand, with gestures, "take my boots, me," he adds in tears, "die: too old."

He had managed to gather a few French words to act out this great performance. I cannot let him walk away with my pierced shoes, for his look is so pleading.

It is finally without exchanging a word that we return to Luzy, each in our own shoes. Operation failed, definitely failed!

23 September

Any day now, the Maquis must be disbanded; but those who wish may enlist in the Army and continue the fight against the Germans, in a regular unit.

To close the chapter of our "celebrations", the 5th Company was sent to Lanty. There again, they wanted to honour the maquisards, prove to them that they had faith in them, and tell them all the joy they felt at seeing a French flag once again at an official ceremony. For the inhabitants of Lanty, our presence was tangible, formal and irrefutable evidence of the defeat of the invaders. It marked both the end of a nightmare, and the announcement of the approaching and much hoped for return of their prisoner sons.

In the afternoon, while the heat of a blazing sun made a doubly potent brew of the good wine which was so generously provided, two farmers asked to be received by the lieutenant.

"There are Germans," they said, "hiding near a pond 2km away. They were spotted several times prowling around farms, no doubt looking for some chickens to steal. And as they are armed ..."

The lieutenant quickly made a decision; he needed volunteers. This time I was finally going to get my Germans, at the very last. Michel did not say no. Jim felt like stretching his legs. We were soon a dozen under orders from Révol.

As our only ammunition was the bullets contained in the clips of our weapons, we made a collection between two tangos among friends and acquaintances, who preferred to stay and dance to the sound of the accordion in the classrooms. They were not rich pickings, but we certainly wouldn't have to fight a long battle!

"The Germans shouldn't put up too much of a fight," the sergeant said. After a cautious walk, we reached the edge of the woods; there, Révol explained his plan.

"I know the local area quite well. We'll set the machine gun up against the long edge of the woods, to catch them if they attempt to escape through the fields. With six men, I'll try and drive them in your direction, while Speedboat and Will go round the wood on the other side, just in case they decide to get away through the pond. You never know: maybe they like water lilies!"

Slipping along the path, we felt as though we were taking part in a wild boar hunt, ready to dispatch this new breed into another kingdom if we had to.

We played for a good while with blackberries and wild roses, before reaching the other side of the wood. It was then that suddenly, we were caught in fire from automatic weapons. Flattened side by side on the ground, covered with leaves and branches ripped off by the bursts of gunfire, we quickly exchanged a few sentences.

"You okay?"

"Yes. They almost had us, the bastards!"

"The Germans have spotted us, but Révol is going to take them from the other side. If they retreat through the fields, we will shoot them down like rabbits!"

"OK."

Nothing moved, no further shots: this time, we would at last have our fight.

I felt as though I occupied a huge volume, and yet my buttocks were probably barely to be seen above the rut where I had dived when I heard the screech of the first bullets.

"Michel!"

"What?"

"What if we tried to take them prisoner?"

"It depends ... If there are lots of them, we might have to shoot. We'll see!"

Our wait was short lived. Révol's laughter and a lot of shouting resounded nearby.

Part of the Révol Group. From left to right: Sergeant Révol, Dentelle (Lace), Jim, Vedette (Speedboat), Aiguille (Needle), Volonté (Will), Drap (Cloth), Rosario, Cargo.

They probably wanted to signal their presence to the boys on the machine gun. Cautiously, we half got up. The sergeant appeared a few hundred metres away, and saw us kneeling. We must have looked gormless, with our guns in our hands, because he shouted to us:

"The evening prayer is over, you can stand up!"

A ragged individual was following him. From the back pocket of his thread-bare jacket hung the bobbing head of a dead rabbit. He was a poacher. So our farmers' Germans had turned into a tramp, who took advantage of the circumstances to operate unchallenged.

Now Jim turned up with his machine gun. He was the one who had showered us with bullets all too hastily, when we had reached the long edge of the wood without realising it, for we were bent double.

We returned empty-handed once again. No, it was impossible! Sickened, I stood still for a while, pondering this new twist of fate.

The sun had just set when our procession, less triumphant than *Peter and the Wolf*, set out to return to Lanty. As we walked alongside the pond, a couple of ducks slowly flew up. I shouldered my rifle and fired. Indifferent, with their long necks stretched out, they continued their flight. To kill a duck with a bullet, you needed luck! I fired two more bullets in their direction; the shots and the kick of the rifle cooled me down a little.

"Will you stop it! Are you mad?" shouted Révol.

Why was I so disappointed? Because my last hope of fighting had just vanished? What was I hoping for? That I'd really kill a man? Kill a man! To prove what?

Révol was right; I was mad, quite mad! I had to stifle my disappointment right away, and listen to other voices.

"Wisdom has built her house, she has sculpted seven columns. She has killed her animals, prepared her wine and set her table. She has sent her servants and proclaimed from the heights of the city: come and eat my bread and drink the wine I have prepared! Leave your madness and you will live: follow the path of intelligence."

But for the past 6 years, men have not been able to hear.

24 September

In an instant, the cat had ransacked everything with its mad mechanical paws. The old woman was crying now over her terracotta pots with their limp and injured flowers. She had planned to take them to the cemetery that very afternoon, to her dead one.

When one has nurtured flowers with love, with an end of life love, with an eye for the important things, for the essential details, the colours are probably more delicate, and the stems more slender. She was calling me as a witness of what she considered a catastrophe.

Luzy celebrates its liberation, late September 1944. Captain Kenneth Mackenzie, alias Captain Baptist, makes a speech. Next to him is Abbot Bonin, who has happily switched his battle dress for his cassock.

Now that the Germans have left, I thought, life will resume quickly, very quickly. One will no longer mourn a tortured son, a son who will not return, but a faded flower, an unsuccessful afternoon, a kiss stolen by another. The tree will become a tree again. We will notice that birds nest in its branches. Only the man will not change. He will carry on living with his joys and his sorrows. He will carry on being good or bad.

In the beginning, did Cain not kill Abel?

25 September

The great adventure is over!

On my way to the marketplace, where companies will be gathered for the last time, I think about these last few years, and especially the recent months. In significant circumstances, do we always review things, and draw conclusions as at the end of a well-balanced essay?

What have I done? Very little, in short. I have not encountered real fear, nor the intoxication of fighting; at most a few hours' waiting for a few minutes' anxiety. Others have done more, so much more. These are the ones that Captain Baptist will include in the victory. I go to a prize-giving ceremony without glory or certificate of merit.

"Soldier Verneret," they will say to me. "Where are your dead, your prisoners? Did you never fight?"

I will defend myself.

"But, Captain, it is fate which did not give me a single sign, not the slightest gesture. The brute! I came to the Maquis precisely for that reason, to fight; and then I waited for a long time, stupidly. You, Captain, are lucky to be a captain, to have jumped with your parachute, to have hunted, to have chased; to have fought, and to have won. You have been a useful tool in the hands of fate!"

However, Baptist spoke to us not as a glorious soldier, but simply, with his heart.

"The task accomplished," he said, "was great, and I associate all the maquisards with our victory. It is thanks to the obscure and sometimes unimportant work accomplished by each and every one of us that the Maquis was able to live and fight. Let all of us be united as brothers around the same table in the joy of our hearts and the triumph of our weapons, whether we enlisted at the start of war or nearer the end."

Yes, Baptist was right: the main thing was that we were finally gathered together. That our sufferings were different did not matter any more. War is not necessarily a fight, deaths, injuries; it is also sometimes a mere wait. And then, we are not all made to be heroes!

Part II: Twenty-Five Years Later

It would be fair to suggest that when one joins a movement, one knows its aims and its origins.

On rereading my notebooks, however, I realised that I knew nothing about the history and background of the group of Resistance fighters I had joined.

At Les Fréchots, having become a cog within the mysterious machine, I had not obtained any further information on the Louis Maquis. I was still none the wiser on the evening when we disbanded and I handed over my gun and grenades to the officer sitting in front of the blackboard, instead of the schoolmaster, in Luzy's small school.

My ignorance was either due to indifference (I must not have considered it important at the time), or the feeling that I was unable to learn more. Some 25 years later, reasonably, I am intensely curious.

I have therefore sought out some of the men who initiated this epic in the Nevers area, and having finally found them, I learned how, on the mountains of the Morvan, first the Resistance, and then the Louis Maquis were born.

The interviews that I report here reveal the faces of brave men, whose common feature is without doubt a great generosity, combined with undeniable qualities of the heart.

When one has repeatedly risked one's life, selfishness disappears. This is quite clear.

Interview with Abbot Bonin

HV: Colonel Roche said in Luzy, in 1946: The Louis Maquis was the finest and the strongest of all the maquis in the Nivernais and the Morvan. As maquisards, we would certainly not deny it.

AB: At the time of the Liberation, we had at least five companies at the camp.

HV: Yes. I was in the 5th.

AB: There were 2,000 men, maybe more, in Les Fréchots and the village groups. This was an extraordinary burgeoning from a few underground elements! I remember the first meetings in Millay, in my rectory office, with Lieutenant Botté and a few local young people, and then, later, with Louis after he had been parachuted in, in 1943.

HV: So the future maquis had two leaders?

AB: It could not have two leaders, you see. So Louis thought of doing something in the Nevers area, but that soon proved impossible because of the very active surveillance by the Gestapo. Finally, he came back to the Luzy area, and it was Botté, known as Armand, who went to Franche-Comté.

HV: Louis had arrived alone at your place?

AB: Yes. He came alone, on a motorcycle. He had learned that I belonged to the Resistance and he wanted me to help hide Captain Baptist who was about to be parachuted in. I set him up in Lavault, near Millay, at Madame d'Escrienne's house. Then Louis built his first team, and they went to Poil, near Pierrefitte, but they quickly sought somewhere else, because it was unsafe there.

HV: Were there many of them at this time?

AB: Oh, maybe thirty, with the Resistance core in Étang-sur-Arroux and the Luzy men: Passard, Pinet, the station manager, and Berthin, the surveyor. It was Berthin who found the final location of Les Fréchots. They were very well off indeed there, and close to home!

HV: How was recruitment carried out later on?

AB: They drafted a mobilisation poster, which asked young people to enlist rather than going to the STO (*Service du travail obligatoire*), the compulsory labour service in Germany. They came from Millay, Larochemillay, Poil, Sémelay.

HV: From Nevers too, since Michel and I were from Nevers, and we hadn't read the posters!

AB: Yes. From Nevers, Bourbon, even Paris. Many passed through my "recruitment office" until the day when I had to hurriedly join the Maquis myself.

HV: But you had never been suspected beforehand?

AB: Suspected, certainly. Questioned, no. At the time they came to arrest me, I fled. I left through the rear of the rectory. The Germans had come with two trucks. That was the evening that they were attacked near the chateau; they lost one or two men. A Gestapo man had come to the area to investigate. He was hoping to arrest both me and Madame d'Escrienne. In the event, he ended up a prisoner of the Maquis. I was at the camp, next to Captain Louis, when he was questioned; he confessed everything, not realising that it was I, Abbot Bonin, carefully listening to his confession. How could he recognise me wearing British battledress rather than a cassock?

HV: When was this, approximately?

AB: About 15 August 1944. They wanted to shoot him. I intervened and asked that he be made prisoner. At the Liberation, he was sent to Pougues, and then, I don't know what became of him.

HV: For you, as a priest, was it serious to allow a German to be shot if he had been found guilty?

AB: He was not even German. He was a man from Alsace in civilian clothes, who had tried to mingle with the population in order to spy on us more efficiently. Yes, it was bad to shoot a man, but one must remember the circumstances: we were completely exhausted. We had suffered so much. Some of our people had been routed several times. Men had been killed, shot, often after having been tortured; for us, it was a matter of survival. More than that even.

HV: Survival was made up of important things and small details too. They say that before joining the Maquis, and despite the ban, you continued to ring your bells every Sunday?

AB: Yes. The few Germans who were in the area must have thought that I had permission. It is true that they did not hang around here. They thought that the Maquis was 25,000 men strong. This explains why they would never attack it head on. If they had known that we were only 2,000 …

HV: Do you remember that it was our group, the Révol Group, who had built the wooden altar on which you said mass, at the camp?

AB: Yes, yes, I remember. There was also a young seminarian from Autun.

HV: Maybe, but he did not belong to our group.

AB: I'll tell you something that will surprise you, I expect: I met more serious worshippers amongst the maquisards than during the Phoney War 1939–40, while I was a military chaplain!

HV: Captain Louis and Lieutenant Baptist were probably Protestants?

AB: Captain Louis was definitely Catholic.

HV: He was Catholic?

AB: Yes. Baptist was Protestant but very "right-minded"!

HV: I would be very interested in getting information on Louis' English family through Baptist, and the reasons for the formation of a maquis in Morvan supported by the War Office.

AB: But Louis was French, not English! Having reached England in 1943, he had joined the British Army and was assigned to Colonel Buckmaster's network. He was parachuted in a first time as a lieutenant, I believe.

HV: Louis was French? Ah! I was convinced … Well, everyone in the Maquis believed that he was English!

AB: No. He was born in Nice, where his father was an architect. Baptist, Philip, André were English, but not Louis. Baptist, in fact, was Scottish. You remember Philip? Taken in by a family near the Montarons?

HV: Yes. He was my age, 19 years old.

AB: It was an army of young people!

HV: They say that Louis went out rarely, initially. Was this true?

AB: Yes, maybe, at the beginning. He remembered having been arrested and imprisoned. He saw Germans everywhere.

HV: How old was he when he died?

AB: Twenty-four, I believe. He was reckless, in essence, Louis. Obviously, at the beginning, we sensed a man who would give nothing away about himself. We even wondered whether he would do anything. And then, when he felt that he had sufficient men and equipment, despite the extent of his responsibilities at such a young age, then he was really dynamic, and even reckless. Yes, reckless!

HV: Why did Louis create village groups like the one in Chiddes? I remember Monsieur Rasse, from the Chiddes Group; we had drunk a good bottle at his place before joining the Maquis!

AB: Village groups were necessary to keep in touch with the communities, ensure communication, deliver supplies to the camp. They played a very important part, these village groups, and they were sometimes better placed to respond quickly than the maquisards. They were really very valuable links.

HV: At the Liberation, in Millay, they must have given you quite a reception!

AB: Well, the Liberation of Millay was actually quite sensational, the rest much less, when "those who had done nothing" wanted to claim certain great actions as theirs. But that is nothing to do with the Louis Maquis!

Interview with Émile Passard

HV: Being one of the oldest resistants from the Luzy area, you must have some remarkable memories about the Louis Maquis?

EP: I'll tell you. We did so much, so many different things. But remembering, just like that …

HV: You should have written your impressions down day by day, or soon after the war. That's what I did when I was at Les Fréchots.

EP: You weren't in the Louis Maquis. You were too young!

HV: No, I wasn't too young. You will see, as I did just now, at Madame Berthin's, that I am mentioned on the service records.

EP: So, we must have had your papers at home. We had all the maquisards' papers here.

HV: Yes, I was asked for them when I arrived at the camp. But was it wise to centralise all these identity papers at Luzy in this way? It might have caused terrible reprisals if they had been discovered.

EP: Oh, they were well hidden! The Germans did actually come here, and searched everywhere; they even took away empty crates, but no documents. However, we had been warned of their visit.

The maquisards had arrested a high-up German, who had confessed that the Gestapo was to raid our place that very evening. As the maquis was directly connected to the Luzy Post Office, we had been warned in time.

Talking about the Post Office, I don't know whether you know that Bondoux and I were the ones who blew it up?

The Montarons Maquis, I think, had already planted three or four plastic explosives there, but they did nothing at all! So Captain Louis said to me: "Old chap, it's imperative that it should blow up."

"What must blow up?"

"The Post Office."

"Didn't it? For God's sake, what went wrong?"

"They failed."

"Don't worry, I'll sort it out."

So I went to find Bondoux and I said to him: "I need you to tell me exactly where the wires enter the Post Office."

It was absolutely essential that we should blow it up, do you see? The Germans used this place.

Bondoux said to me: "Here is exactly what must be done."

I replied: "We'll do it. Don't worry!"

"When?"

"Tonight."

We were in disguise, Jules Bondoux and I. We were supposed to go at 9 o'clock in the evening, and what do I see coming? Baptist and Lieutenant "Leon" escorted by about 30 fellows.

As soon as I recognised Mackenzie (Baptist), I went to meet them and asked them why they had come. "Captain Louis insisted on our coming." After what had happened, he feared that the Germans might come back, do you see?

Then we got down to business. It did not take long. We placed a big ladder against the wall; it must have been quite 10m high. We cut all the wires, and then we poured some spirit of salts, you know, some acid, something like that.[8]

HV: Hydrochloric acid?

EP: What?

HV: Hydrochloric?

EP: Yes, something like that.

HV: Not something close, if it was spirit of salts, believe me … I got a chemical engineering qualification, a few years ago!.

EP: Ah! Good … Ah! Yes … So it was that. We wanted everything to be damaged, rusty, so that they could no longer recognise the wires; because they each had their colour.

HV: You did it very scientifically.

EP: Listen, it was no joke, eh! We poured acid in there like crazy. I can still remember poor old mother somebody …[9]

HV: Who?

EP: Durand's wife. She was crying: "Oh, they'll kill us all." And there was her wretched husband saying to her as he hid behind the door: "But, do be quiet. There's no threat to us!" Ah! They were frightened!

---

[8] *Esprit-de-sel* (spirit of salts) was the old French name for hydrochloric acid for domestic use.

[9] "Poor" is used in the Morvan instead of "late" or "deceased".

Then the maquisards who were there repeated: "Come on, don't worry Mother Durand!"

HV: Were you at Les Fréchots with the maquisards at that time?

EP: No, I went up from time to time, but it was here, in Luzy, that I received orders. I only stayed there at the end.

HV: At what point did you join the Resistance?

EP: Oh, almost at the beginning. Before Louis was parachuted in, we had a French officer here: Armand. He took care of derailing the trains. At that time, I supplied the Maquis from Luzy to the borders of the Jura. Although I am a mechanic, my house was the largest butcher's shop in the area!

HV: You also stored explosives and equipment?

EP: Yes, I had a little of everything. At the beginning, I worked with Armand. Poor chap, he was killed. He was quite someone, you know. Armand was quite someone! Here's how I met him: he had been wandering around Luzy and the neighbourhood for 10 days, chucking grenades, just like that, at trains loaded with equipment, straw. So, you see, there was fire everywhere spreading in the wind. Others unscrewed the tracks.

There was a group here at Luzy, and another at Étang. They lived where they could: one day here, one day there, one day in the woods. They hid. One evening, I was outside on a bench; there goes my Réty, who says to me: "Monsieur Passard, I have something to ask you."

"What is it? Well, what is it then?"

"Listen ... can I trust you?"

"My goodness! And can I trust you?"

"Well. We want to set up a maquis in the area. There is an officer with us, but he needs putting up. Sometimes, he is over here. Two days later, he is over there. He doesn't know where to hide. He must be put up somewhere. You are from Luzy and you know everybody in town: you could find us someone trustworthy.

"Goodness! This is no joke!"

"No. This is serious ... very serious."

"Okay, I think I know someone."

"Who?"

"Me. Well, if we are going to resist, let's resist. But, no jokes, eh? We two know, but no one else must!" You understand: two, three, four people get to know and then you've had it! It really wasn't a joke!

"Don't worry. His name is Armand. Can he come tonight?"

"Yes, at 9."

At 9 sharp, he was here. I had said to my wife: "There is a chap staying with us tonight. Put him in the room next to ours."

When he arrived, I asked if he had eaten. "Yes, I've eaten." And he stayed. For 3 months! In fact, he did not always stay in Luzy. He left, he returned, he received orders from the War Office, he went to England and also to Switzerland. He was a real daredevil. One day, he said to me: "I don't want to work with them anymore. I am French, I want to work with the French. I've had enough." And he kicked a crate of machine guns. "I'm going back to Franche-Comté."

Then I said: "What can I do with all that?"

"Just hand them over to Pinet, the station master. Thomas will pick them up in 2 or 3 days. Or you can keep them: you're in, now, after all!"

Before leaving, Armand had said to me: "They are going to parachute someone in quite soon." It was Captain Louis.

HV: So Armand brought Louis to you?

EP: Yes. He went to pick him up, and then, one evening, they arrived together, just like that, unexpectedly. There were three people in the house, including my own nephew, and another young man who had not gone to the STO. It was 9 or 10 o'clock. We were playing cards. So my Armand comes in, with five or six huge men, almost 2m in height, and Louis. We went into the next room. "Let me introduce the man who is to replace me," Armand said. He was not big.

I said to myself:."I don't know this young man. I don't know whether he is any good." He was actually thinking the same thing.

After that, I had to go back to the card game and Francis asked me: "Who are those fellows?"

"They are boys who have come to ask me about making charcoal. The smallest is a boy I know, who would like to set up a kind of factory."

Louis stayed with us. He took Armand's place. Immediately, he gave me a revolver with magazines full of bullets, and said to me: "I am not moving for 8 days".

Initially, he had no appetite. He didn't know how things were going to work out. My wife and I, we did everything we could to put him at ease, but he was worried.

There were a dozen Germans who were staying not far from here; they came from time to time to repair their stuff in my workshop. One day, they came in loudly, straight into the shop, just as my Louis was coming down the stairs in his pyjamas. When he saw them, he jumped back up five or six steps at a time. He was not accustomed to rubbing shoulders with Germans in uniform, but I had to talk to them to try and get information.

Sometimes the Germans let off flares, and no one knew why. One evening, I asked one of my neighbours who knew a few bits of French: "Yesterday, pretty fireworks ... Nice, eh?"

"Ah, ya, ya ... nice fireworks."

"Why?"

"Why? Ah, ya ... Communication with other post to signal passage British planes." Thus, isolated posts were all informed, and we were too!

HV: Did Louis have to ask London for weapons early on?

EP: Yes, and the first parachute drop occurred on the property of Monsieur Anginieur, from Magny, at Le Breu. Louis said to me almost immediately: "The parachute drop was almost certainly spotted; there were Germans patrolling in the area. We'll need to find another drop zone, and, in the meantime, we should move the containers."

HV: Was this first shipment of weapons important?

EP: Oh, there were about thirty containers. The boys had hidden them in bushes. You know Poil well, Le Breu, is right nearby, a small farm, in the woods.

HV: Had Armand ever received a parachute drop?

EP: No. For what reason? I do not know. Then Louis said to me: "We need to find a car to move everything." I still had 10l of petrol that I kept carefully, and an unused car in the garage.

I immediately said to him: "I will go at 9." At 9 o'clock, he too was there. It was already dark. I don't remember exactly, but I believe that it was snowing a little; in any case, it was cold.

We arrived at Le Breu cautiously because of the driving prohibition, and to avoid using too much petrol. I refrained from sudden acceleration. The boys were waiting for us. They had already moved all the containers from the wood down to the road. Then, in five or six trips, Louis and I transported all the parachuted equipment in the small van. Then we had to take the containers back up to the caretaker's empty house at the Château de Pierrefitte. It was not an easy matter. We managed without a hitch and without attracting the attention of the Germans who were patrolling in the area. Fortunately I knew the small roads better than they did. We got through.

HV: And how did the others get to Pierreffitte?

EP: By bicycle.

HV: Were there many of them at this time with Louis?

EP: About ten, in the derailment team that Armand had set up. Armand had said to the station master and others: "Here, let me introduce your new leader: he is Captain Louis." I don't know if he was captain at the time.

He was perhaps only a lieutenant. Yes. He must have been a captain. Yes. We called him Captain.

That was the night that I met Baptist, in the caretaker's house. When I realised what we looked like in there, I said to Louis: "Listen, surely you aren't thinking of staying here: everyone will see you! There are people who are going to do the ploughing. There are scores of people who will go by on their bicycles. Don't stay here!"

HV: You had never seen Baptist before that night?

EP: No. He was already at Madame d'Escrienne's, but I saw him at Pierrefitte for the first time. I even slept beside him.

HV: Did you sleep well? Anxiety may have outweighed fatigue?

EP: We were exhausted, you see! It was quite something, what we had done! We were fed up. Then Louis said to us before going to bed: "I will give you a little tea." I said to him:

"Is that all you've got to give us?"

"There is chocolate too."

"Okay, so let's have your chocolate!" Because in the containers, there were a few small things like that for them!

Before I fell asleep, I said to Louis again: "Don't stay here."

"Yes, but where can I go?"

I thought about this again the next day, and the day after, then I met Jules Bondoux. He was distributing leaflets and newspapers and because of that, he saw many people. He said to me: "Monsieur Passard, I know someone who would like to join the Resistance."

"Who?"

"Berthin."

"The surveyor?"

"Yes."

"That's quite a scoop, old chap!"

As he was a surveyor, I said to myself: this is a man who knows the area like the back of his hand. Louis was waiting for me. Immediately, I said to him: "I know someone who will certainly help us out. He would like to join us, take part in a little Resistance!"

"Okay, go and meet him."

Louis did not have to think twice. Immediately, I jumped on my bike and went to find Berthin. He was not far away, just coming out of the wood.

"Listen to me, I have something to tell you.".

"OK, what is it?".

"First, are you French?".

"I hope so. I hope that I am French!"

"That's good. Listen. We are setting up Resistance in the area. If … if you wanted, we could certainly use your help."

"I ask for nothing better." He added: "Let's go upstairs, because we could be overheard down here!"

"I don't like to speak in front of the ladies.".

"You can be sure that it will remain secret, there is no risk."

All the same, I was ill at ease! What if someone …? Finally, I went up, and explained the matter to him. "The thing is, we have had a parachute drop that we have taken to a safe house."

"Oh, so this is serious!"

"Of course it's serious! Goodness, yes! Could you find us a place to set up a maquis of 250 men, 1,000 if need be?"

Then, I explained to him that Louis, whom he did not know, had received orders from the War Office to organise resistance on the mountains of the Morvan, because it was thought that the Germans would hang on there in case of withdrawal. I then suggested: "Come to my house, so that you can meet Louis."

I had been home for 5 minutes when Berthin arrived. The captain explained to him that he hoped to hide weapons in cemented tanks that roadmen set up on roadsides to keep tar in.

Berthin pulled a face. When Louis had finished his presentation, he replied: "In any case, you should not stay where you are. You'll get executed! It will only take the Germans a week to find you and you will all be shot!" Finally, Berthin said: "I know a place. We can go tomorrow, if you like."

Louis replied: "Why not go there at once!" He was in a hurry!

Berthin had a motorbike; me too – a motorbike that I had given to Louis. Off they went, both of them, not on the same route of course! They met at Les Fréchots. The only people left were an old man and his wife, and there were several abandoned houses.

When Louis came back that evening, he said at once: "Well, my friend, what a find! There is everything we need there to house the men. We'll be sheltered. There are empty houses; there is water for washing, and drinking water for cooking!"

Louis was happy. I believe that he kissed me! He said to me: "Oh, it's wonderful. Now, let's put up a poster. We need men." I was beginning to discover the new Louis, the Louis who took risks.

Finally posters were displayed, even in the Town Hall in Luzy. I'm not sure, but I think Berthin did it.

HV: Was it from this point on that the numbers of the maquis suddenly increased?

EP: Yes, men arrived from everywhere. From Luzy, of course, from Autun, gendarmes from Saône-et-Loire: there were 250–300 gendarmes with us; they were a company. Men were coming from Bourbon. There were young people who came to see me, and said to me: "We want to join the maquis."

I replied: "But I have nothing to do with the maquis!".

"Ah! We were told that you do." Then, finally, I took them. Once, I took fifteen at a time. Sometimes, I made them wait. I hid them where I could. Often, I took them by road, beyond the bridge.

HV: Fortunately there were quite a few airdrops at the time, because arming everyone must have been quite an undertaking!

EP: Yes, but it was dangerous to do a parachute drop in the same place. We had to find a new field. I found one that seemed good to me, not far from a small café I knew in the middle of nowhere.

I said to Louis: "Come with me, to see if it's suitable." There were coppices here, coppices there. It was a pasture, and not well maintained, you see!

So I take my Louis. We stop at the café first for a drink; you know how it is – sometimes we have to invent stories so as not to attract people's attention. In short, I wanted to chat for a bit with the owners.

Louis said to me: "I am not really thirsty."

"Well then, we'll eat some ham; I know she has good ham. I know this lady has good ham."

We go in, and I say: "Please will you make us a nice little ham omelette." And I add: "Are there any snails, round here? Because we're here to gather some!"

She said: "Oh, yes! There are!" So off we went. Obviously, we couldn't care less about snails, but we pretended to look for them with a stick, when in fact we were checking out the field.

Finally, Louis says: "It's very good. We must have the next parachute drop here. There won't just be snails in the area!"

HV: Some containers were, apparently, reserved for officers. The colour of the parachute gave information about the nature of the content, and black parachutes were supposed to mean the dispatch of money, or so the rumour ran.

EP: Maybe so! Talking about money, while Louis stayed with us in Luzy, he went off one day towards Toulouse, and I borrowed the bike he used sometimes to run errands. I left it in front of the hairdresser's, and all over the place, before I realised that there were 500,000 francs in banknotes in a small black pouch in one pannier and, in the other, loose, several hand grenades! For 3 days, I swear to God, I rode around with all that! I even think that the bike once spent the night outside!

When Louis arrived, he said: "Where's the bike?"
"There." He looks and finds the money and the grenades.
"Goodness, how careless of me!"
"I know; I rode around on the bike for three days!"

HV: You used to hide or carry weapons, didn't you?
EP: Yes. There were some in the garage, in the straw, and in crates, under boards. I left everything in a real mess on purpose. It was filthy! One day, the Germans came to commandeer my garage; it would be well suited, you see, to repairing machine guns or rifles. They made a kind of inventory; there were steel plates in a corner.

"For sale, sir?"
"No. Not for sale." They were big blokes; they drank and ate well. There was a captain and there were men, with necks as thick as you please! The captain sat on boards, and had taken out his notepad. I was thinking: if you knew what you've got your bottom on!

HV: This was no time to be afraid, and yet ...
EP: Ah, if I had changed my attitude or changed my way of life during those years, I would not be here today with you. We had to behave as if the Germans weren't in Luzy.

Your cousin Alphonse Perriault also hid weapons where he lived, in his butcher's shop. And something very strange happened to him. The weapons were hidden between the ceiling of a first-floor bedroom and the floor of the attic. Under the weight of the machine guns and the guns, the ceiling gave way one night, luckily falling at the foot of the bed where his daughter was sleeping. All this equipment had therefore to be moved out as a matter of urgency. Alphonse called on two resistants of our group, and as soon as the curfew was lifted, they made several trips to the cemetery with an old cart pulled by a bicycle. The cart had a false bottom, and tools, tiles and an old ladder were piled on top. At the cemetery, the weapons and ammunition were hidden in an old chapel. I can even tell you that the chapel belonged to the Nonat family. Nowadays, it would be considered a desecration.

We took risks every day. And then, I killed ... how many? At least fifty or sixty animals, in the garage. Sometimes the blood ran out and onto the pavement.

Right at the beginning Armand had said to me: "My boys in the Jura are starving. If only we could make sausages, smoked sausages!" He knew that I was killing animals you see.

He was from the east, or thereabouts, and he was used to eating smoked sausage. So I said to him: "Don't worry, we'll make smoked sausage."

A little further on, I had another small workshop that was accessed by three or four steps. I thought that it would be possible to smoke meat there.

I killed the animals with Father Prébin, who was a former butcher from Luzy. He was the one who told me that Voyot had a sausage-making machine which he did not use any more.

Then we collected some sheep gut, and we made sausages with veal, mostly. You see, pigs screamed too loudly. It would have alerted the whole neighbourhood. So we sometimes made up to 50kg of sausage. Afterwards, it had to be smoked. We hung it all under a large canopy. We sealed it, and then I got pine sawdust at the sawmill and in the woods, juniper, herbs, and I don't remember what else, and then we smoked.

Armand was pleased. He said: "My boys will be happy, and what's more, smoked sausage keeps well! It will last them a long time!"

HV: You had many trades, all in all? Mechanic, garage owner, butcher, smuggler, hotelier, maquisard …

EP: Ah, during the war, you know, we had to do everything!

Interview with Kenneth Mackenzie ("Baptist")

HV: When I arrived in London, this morning, by plane, I was thinking about the journey you made in the opposite direction 26 years ago, to come and help us in the Morvan. I was wondering what had led the War Office to send its officers to take charge of a maquis in the heart of France.

I was also thinking about the very varied training that you had to endure to prepare for such a complex mission. One does not become a radio operator, a parachutist and a maquisard in one day!

We could therefore talk about all this, if you are willing, but first of all I would like to ask you if you knew Louis before arriving at Les Fréchots?

KM: Yes. We were in the same group, but I didn't know that I was going to be with him later in France when we trained. Louis had been trained as an organiser. I myself arrived in France to replace a radio operator who had just been caught by the Gestapo. After having passed out as an artillery officer, I had undergone a year of specialised training, followed by training in radio transmission.

HV: Had you become a parachutist, meanwhile?

KM: Yes, but we were so well trained physically, that we only needed 5 or 6 weeks to be ready.

HV: Did you do numerous jumps?

KM: Four or five, I think. Yes, the sixth was the good one, but before arriving in the Morvan, I had made a trip over France. A pointless trip, in February 1944, as I was unable to make contact with the group in the Pyrenees, where I was meant to go. So I came back to England, and we tried again only a month later because of the moon: we had to choose times when the moon was full, so that I only arrived in March 1944, a few months before the Normandy landing.

HV: Whereas Louis had been parachuted in at the end of 1943?

KM: Yes. Louis came to pick me up in the Pyrenees, because he had no radio, and without a radio he was very handicapped.

HV: Were you appointed for this mission because you spoke perfect French?

KM: Yes, certainly. My mother was French, but I had a slight Scottish accent; I rolled my Rs. This is how I could pass, in the eyes of the Germans at least, for a perfect Morvandiau! It is perhaps one of the reasons for my coming to this area.

HV: Did they only take volunteers?

KM: Absolutely; at the last moment, I could have refused. Even as I boarded the plane.

HV: Were there many of you in this special training camp?

KM: In the radio section, we were seventeen. I am one of the three who returned! The others were killed or taken by the Germans. After they had been captured, they were interrogated, tortured and then, some time later, shot.

HV: Even though they were British officers, in uniform?

KM: We were not recognised as British officers! Except, perhaps, towards the end of the war, then the Germans were inclined to treat their prisoners better.

HV: Yes, they were actually beginning to fear possible reprisals themselves.

KM: At the beginning, we didn't have uniforms, just armbands as a distinctive sign.

HV: When you were parachuted in, did you know that you were to work with Louis?

KM: Before leaving London, Colonel Maurice Buckmaster, the head of the group to which I belonged, had said to me: "Do you want to work with Louis?"

I replied: "Certainly. He is a very intelligent man." And then, I felt that we could really count on him. So I said that I would be very pleased to be with him.

HV: How come Louis served in the British Army, rather than with Free France, and de Gaulle?

KM: It was at his own request. He was accepted. After undergoing tests, of course!

HV: In order to ensure that he was not a German spy?

KM: Yes. From time to time, so-called volunteers were uncovered.

HV: Had the decision to form a maquis in the Morvan actually been taken by the War Office?

KM: Definitely. The War Office knew the situation in France quite well. They knew that the parachuting in of officers trained in guerrilla warfare, with radio transmitters, would facilitate the gathering at strategic points of the many willing individuals of the Resistance who were somewhat scattered, in some areas at least.

HV: Did Louis choose to come to the Luzy area, where he met Lieutenant Armand?

KM: It was certainly the War Office who decided, according to needs and geographical location.

HV: Which region were you parachuted into?

KM: Into Ariège, about 30 or 40km south of Pamiers; and then I was sent to Toulouse, where I stayed for 10 days before returning to the Nièvre. I arrived at the small station in Luzy by train, and I spent my first Morvan evening in a nearby property. Monsieur Pinet met me in Luzy.

HV: After that you went to Madame d'Escrienne, didn't you?

KM: That is correct. The very next day, they bought me a bicycle, a beautiful bicycle.

HV: Signed Passard, no doubt?

KM: Definitely. We left during the night, for Lavault, where Madame d'Escrienne took me in. I lived there until the time of the landing. Four or five days beforehand, I received a radio message telling me to be on my guard, and leave Lavault.

HV: Did you have a radio set at Madame d'Escrienne's? Were you in direct contact with London?

KM: Yes, but not from the chateau. I would never send messages from a French house. I had five transmitters that I left in different places, in the woods of the surrounding area. Whenever I did a broadcast, I hid the set in a hole under ferns. My contact hours with London were irregular and I changed radio set and frequency at each transmission. I felt safer.

HV: They must have been very small sets, to have so many?

KM: No, they were as big as suitcases: they were about 3ft [90cm] long.

HV: Had they been parachuted in at the same time as you?

KM: I had lost all my transmitters shortly after my arrival in France. We were discovered in Toulouse by the German military police and had to abandon everything: radios and weapons. So we had to send a radio message to London through another group, to ask for new equipment.

HV: How did you manage to escape from the military police?

KM: During our transfer to the Gestapo in Toulouse, Louis and I were sitting in the back between two Germans. At the same moment, we gave them a karate chop before jumping out of the car each on our side. The military police fired in our direction, but we were able to escape. The head of the Toulouse network also fled, by car. The Germans set off in hot pursuit, but as he knew the old districts better than them, he accelerated, and just before a small street, applied the brakes violently while turning into it. He just made it, but the Germans who were following him rolled their car! He joined us only 2 or 3 hours later, a little breathless and pale, naturally. We were all saved, but I no longer had a radio.

HV: What did you transmit, in your first messages sent from the Morvan?

KM: The messages were all about parachute drops.

HV: And what were you doing, meanwhile?

KM: I remained at the chateau. There was plenty to do: I worked hard because I wanted to do my best to help Madame d'Escrienne. At that time, we only ate meat once a week, if at all! It was hard. Fortunately, there were chickens and eggs. Until that time, I had not eaten eggs for very many years, because I had a serious kidney complaint when I was young, and they were forbidden. But as I was so hungry, I tried again without any ill effects, fortunately!

HV: Airdrops of weapons that you received were, I suppose, not just for the Louis Maquis. Were they also for other maquis in the Nivernais?

KM: They were more especially for our maquis, because we had received orders to establish a very large weapons and ammunition dump. But from time to time, we had requests from other maquis. We were careful who we gave weapons to, because there were some groups that were not very committed!

I know that we did help a few maquis when it was worth it, and when we were certain that this would not in the long run create a danger for us.

HV: But then, how did the other maquis in the area — and they were pretty numerous — get their supplies of weapons?

KM: It wasn't easy. But there were other possibilities, other networks. Those of the Free French, or of de Gaulle, for example, also got airdrops. Sometimes, like us, they took weapons from the Germans!

HV: Did you receive your orders directly from London?

KM: Not especially. Most of the actions were left to the initiative of Louis, who decided depending on the urgency. The only guidelines we received sometimes were to attack this or that objective, for example, a factory, a power station, a bridge, rail tracks. But the main goal was, at this time, to form an efficient group of soldiers who could harass the enemy behind its lines in case the German resistance remained strong after the landing. The war was not yet over, we needed to be able to last for months, or even years!

When we undertook a mission, we always did so as far away as possible from villages, and even from isolated farms to avoid immediate reprisals on the population.

HV: What do you call "as far as possible from the maquis"?

KM: Up to 40 or 50km. We were very well organised. It was Passard who dealt with transport. All kinds of trucks and cars had been requisitioned against reimbursable coupons after the war.

By the time of the Liberation, we had amassed some sixty vehicles. We were therefore in a strong position to attack a long way away from Les Fréchots, so as not to risk the premature discovery of our maquis..These were the instructions of the War Office.

Once, one of our lieutenants attacked a German car, contrary to orders and close to the camp. He killed all the occupants, but there was a heavy artillery regiment following behind. So we just had time to remove the remains of the car, and all traces of the fighting. Very soon afterwards, the regiment arrived and passed by without realising anything, fortunately, otherwise it might well have been a direct attack on the camp with artillery, rockets and flamethrowers.

HV: There was serious fighting on the road to Autun, wasn't there?

KM: Yes, towards the end. As the Germans came through in ever-increasing numbers, we reported troop movements to London, giving the maximum amount of information such as the number of men, the type of equipment, the speed of convoys, and so on.

One day, at our request, two or three RAF Mustangs came to deal with them. But beforehand, we had mined all adjacent roads. When the Mustangs arrived, they cleared the road for 20km up to Autun. Not a single tank, nor a single German vehicle, was able to escape, as those who tried to flee on the side roads were blown up by our mines.

Here's an anecdote: the Morvandiaux didn't like to lose their wheat! At that time, almost during the battle, some farmers insisted on going into their fields with their carts. One or two did manage to pass, fortunately for them, without stepping on mines. What a strange idea! Those Morvandiaux are as stubborn as the Scots!

HV: Since we decided when to attack, we generally lost few men in the fighting, didn't we?

KM: One day, we came close to losing a lot of men! A group of thirty had been surrounded by the Germans in a kind of ravine; that was the day that Dr Benoist came to treat the wounded. There were some sixty Germans or more around them when we received their radio call at the camp, which was 9 or 10km away. I immediately took a group of fifteen double-armed maquisards with me, and we covered the distance in record time. When we arrived, we opened fire with a vengeance, as we advanced and spaced out. The Germans must have thought that we were at least 300. In this way, we managed to free our side, but unfortunately two of them had been killed.

That was when I saw one of our men demonstrate tremendous courage: a small, fair man, he had on his shoulders one of his comrades who was quite seriously injured, and despite heavy fire from the Germans, he managed to save him by carrying him to the edge of the wood. He wouldn't give up! It was extraordinary. Fortunately, he was not shot. I'll never understand how they missed him!

HV: Wasn't there a member of the Gestapo amongst the first Germans taken prisoner?

KM: He wasn't a German, that one: he was from Alsace. There had been a small skirmish near the Château de la Planche, and several days later, the inhabitants were questioned by a man who wanted, supposedly, to become a maquisard. He knew that a maquis existed, since an ambush had taken place a few days earlier. In short, he asked too many questions. So, as soon as we were warned, we sent a sergeant and a man to bring him to Les Fréchots..He was a big, blond fellow, who answered to the name of "Bouquet", but his real name was Strauss. He spoke German and French.

We questioned him pretty closely, because we felt at once that he was not one of ours. For two or three nights, we woke him up around 2 o'clock in the morning and interrogated him at length, noting all his answers, because he gave so many details that we thought he would eventually contradict himself. But he had such a memory, that he related exactly the same facts. He quoted all the places where he had been, the addresses, everything, everything; it was really extraordinary.

After a week, we asked Passard to bring batteries. If, as we thought, he was a Gestapo man who specialised in torture, he would quickly understand how we might use them. If not, he would not get anxious.

As soon as he saw the batteries, he was visibly terrified, and said immediately: "I'll confess everything. But spare me this, I've seen too many Frenchmen undergo this treatment!"

He admitted that he had been sent by the Germans to become a maquisard, and obtain as much information as possible about men, equipment, means of defence and organisation. According to him, the Germans thought that two officers were in charge, one of whom was French and the other British. Supposedly, the British one lived at the intersection of two lines that he had identified by two sets of six numbers on a map. Having checked, we saw that it was the Château de Lavault. So, you can imagine how pleased we were to have captured him before he could denounce Madame d'Escrienne!

Still according to him, the Germans thought that the maquis was 25,000 men strong, whereas in fact, at that time, we had 2,000 men.

HV: This is why they were always reluctant to attack it. But then, didn't they know that the camp was at Les Fréchots?

KM: No, not exactly, they thought that it was in the vicinity. At Luzy, the Germans said: "Over there, there is a very large maquis!" indicating the direction of Mont Beuvray.

HV: What happened to the man from Alsace?

KM: Finally, Louis and I decided to keep him prisoner, rather than have him shot as a spy, because he had mentioned the names of many leading French figures. We thought it could be useful to detain him until the end of the war, but if we had known, we would have had him shot because eventually he only served 18 months in prison, which is not really commensurate!

When he found out that I was British, he came up to me and said: "I've already worked for the British. I gave information on the French naval base in Toulon." He was trying to curry favour. "What business do we have, you and I, with the French?" he added.

HV: Is he not the one who wanted to give information on German prisoners?

KM: No, that was another soldier, a good old fellow, who almost became a maquisard, later on! His comrade had been killed in combat, beside him, and he had been saved because one of our machine guns jammed for a few seconds. That had given him time to put his hands up.

HV: So, he gave you information on other prisoners?

KM: Yes. When we took an SS man, he would say to us: "Careful, this one is bad. Take precautions." or: "That one is an ordinary Wehrmacht soldier, there is no danger." Apart from that, he spent all of his time peeling potatoes in the camp kitchen. He was as happy as Larry, knowing that his war was over.

HV: At the end of the fighting, how many German prisoners were in Les Fréchots?

KM: About 300. We did not particularly want to take prisoners and there were lots of people killed in ambushes. Obviously, we never shot a soldier who surrendered.

HV: Yet there were Germans shot, at the camp!

KM: Only one. He was shot because he had looted and stolen. He was carrying hundreds of thousands of francs.

HV: I remember standing over a German who was digging his grave. Was he the one?

KM: Probably. He was tall and thin! A woman was shot too, do you remember?

HV: No, not at all.

KM: This woman had reported many French families, some of whom were deported to Germany. To prevent her from continuing her deadly work, we abducted her. She told us that she believed in the New Order, and that if she had known that a maquis existed with such discipline and spirit of sacrifice, she could just as well have come with us.

She was an actress by profession. When she found out that she was sentenced to death, she asked to see the priest, and then said: "I am ready to die."

When we went with her down to the wood with the firing squad, we asked her if she wanted her eyes blindfolded. She refused: "I am a French officer's daughter, I know what I did. It is unforgivable. I'll face you and I will die without being blindfolded." She died very bravely.

We couldn't have done otherwise. She had done too much damage. She was responsible for the torture of many French people!

HV: Has anyone any idea of the number of enemy killed in battle by the maquisards?

KM: It's absolutely impossible to say. Some days, nearly 100 soldiers fell in various ambushes. In July, and especially August 1944, there were many fights where it wasn't possible to know the losses suffered by the Germans with any precision, for they always took their dead and wounded away with them.

Remember how the enemy was panic-stricken towards the end? They were shooting in all directions in ravines, on heights, before we fired a single shot. And this was far from the camp, because these soldiers knew that crossing any part of the Morvan was dangerous.

They were shooting to protect themselves, at everything that moved. I remember the road to Autun. What a pathetic spectacle! All we could see were charred trucks, abandoned artillery, burnt-out tanks, all the combined work of both the Mustangs and the maquisards.

Some Germans managed to escape, but many were made prisoner or killed further on.

HV: How did the population react at that time? Do you remember?

KM: Perfectly well. People remained calm, generally. However, some people took advantage of the German defeat to begin settling scores, or to loot. That had to be stopped immediately, by letting it be known that all looters would be shot. One young man was caught, and I had to announce that at 1700hrs the same day, he would be shot!

HV: And was he actually shot?

KM: Yes. He was shot at 1700hrs!

Until the last moment, the lieutenant in charge of the firing squad kept asking me: "Is this a final order, Captain?"

"Yes, it is a final order, and now no need to ask me again!"

Afterwards, whenever I saw this same lieutenant, he accused me of having been too harsh. But from that minute on, there was no looting, no theft. Otherwise, it would have spread like wildfire, wouldn't it?

HV: Did any maquisards take part in retaliation against collaborators, to your knowledge?

KM: No, not as far as I know. In any case, not any of ours. There was great discipline in the maquis, you remember it well!

I found out, later on, that sometimes some married maquisards, or other boys, slipped out of the camp at night to go and see their families or meet a girl somewhere; but it was very dangerous both for us and for them. Moreover, they risked the death penalty, leaving the maquis without an order.

HV: Didn't they just run the risk of having their heads shaved?

KM: No.

HV: This makes me shudder; so I almost got shot? Because on several evenings, I went out with a friend to go and eat an omelette in a little restaurant, thinking that the worst that could happen to us was to get our heads shaved!

KM: Yes, before Louis' death, you'd have got away with it. But later, I had to reinforce discipline. I don't know whether you knew, but there were Germans in the area! And what would you have said, under torture? Confidence for confidence: I went out too, once, with Louis. We went to see Rasse, in Chiddes, for a change of scene. Did you know Rasse?

HV: The wine merchant? Of course!

KM: There was a good core of resistance in Chiddes, Millay and Larochemillay, with Abbot Bonin particularly. I met him a few weeks ago, and he told me about this man from Alsace who belonged to the "Gestapo" and wanted to denounce Madame d'Escrienne. He had also tried to have him arrested. He must have been the same man, the one who was not executed. Abbot Bonin told me he had interceded on his behalf.

In the Morvan, there were some courageous priests, like those in Glux and Montsauche. And many other notable Frenchmen who distinguished themselves with de Lattre, or General Leclerc's 2nd Armoured Division.

HV: You told me earlier that you wore a simple armband like us. But when did you put your uniform on again? I remember you in a British uniform!

KM: I took advantage of a parachute drop to have my battledress "delivered".

The maquisards from the Larochemillay village group, gathered in front of the church at the time of the liberation of Burgundy. All around the Louis Maquis, within a distance of a few kilometres, Captain Louis had established groups of resistance fighters, generally older, who continued to live with their weapons in their villages. They could engage in quick actions against small convoys and report to the maquis more important passings.

HV: In the early days, while he was still in Luzy, do you know whether "Louis" wore disguises? Some say that he did, others that he did not! Some saw him walking round Luzy, limping and leaning on a stick, and then, just a few days later, running in different clothes. On the other hand, I know that he had drawn attention to himself on several occasions. He was not very careful! Someone in my family remembers having met him at a chemist's in Luzy, with a very large sheepskin jacket that he couldn't do up, revealing revolver butts. He must have been a walking arsenal. He wanted an insecticide to get rid of parasites.

"Is it for animals?" the pharmacist asked him.
   "No, for men!"

KM: About the stick, I know that he sprained his ankle from time to time. He had a weak ankle. On the other hand, Louis loved to joke; but I don't think that he dressed up for fun at the time!

HV: When Louis died, you took command. But how did it go when subsequently, Major Fradet joined Les Fréchots? You were only a captain!

KM: When he arrived, I said to him: "Major, I hand over command to you!"

Major Fradet was a career soldier and was wise and cautious. He replied: "This war is not an ordinary war. Furthermore, you know your men better, and I know that they respect you. I shall ask you to remain the leader of this maquis, and I myself shall be at your disposal." Few officers of his rank would have behaved in this way. It was, I think, a difficult decision.

HV: But without doubt a very wise decision, because the Louis Maquis was not a conventional army.

KM: Yes, we had to enforce certain specific points with the maquisards, but we could not demand constant discipline from them, otherwise we would have ended up with a rebellion on our hands.

HV: During these few months with such responsibilities, you must have felt a lot older than your 24 years?

KM: Absolutely. In a few weeks, my hair turned very white! When I got back to England, my temples were entirely white, and then in a few months, everything went back to normal.

HV: How strange!

KM: It was the weariness, the tension. At a certain period, I went almost 2 weeks without sleep; only an hour here, an hour there, randomly, when I could.

HV: Being with other Englishmen must have helped you a little? And Philip. We have not talked about Philip yet. His plane was shot down over the Morvan, wasn't it?

KM: Yes. Philip Fairweather was returning from a raid on Lombardy in Italy. His bomber was actually hit by anti-aircraft defences over Italy and in the end the crew had to bail out near Cercy. The pilot was able to return to England through Spain; he flew again immediately. Unfortunately, he was killed before the armistice. The gunner was beheaded by the tail of the plane when he bailed out. As for Philip, who did not know a word of French, he was immediately taken in by a French family, the Duprilot. They were teachers. They gave him a dictionary, and Philip learned the main verbs. He only spoke in the infinitive. Some time later, he went to a farmer, and then joined a nearby maquis.

One day, they were surrounded by Germans on a farm. Out of thirty-eight maquisards, I believe that only five of them made it. Philip was wounded in the thigh, very close to the femoral artery. He was able to get out through a skylight in the farmhouse, and crawl under a small bridge. He stayed there for 2 or 3 hours, while the Germans went over it again and again! Finally, he managed to reach our maquis with the other survivors.

HV: He knew about your maquis?

KM: Definitely. He had already been there. I was told that there was an Englishman in the area. I was suspicious, and I ordered him to be taken to Les Fréchots. When I heard his Kentish accent, I knew he was actually English, because no German could speak like this.

So, I suggested that he should stay with us for safety's sake. He refused: "I can't abandon the maquis friends who first took me in. It's out of the question! I shall stay with them, but if I need you, I know you're here." I thoroughly liked this 19-year-old boy from that moment on!

Eventually, we took in the five survivors of the maquis, which had been virtually destroyed by the Germans. Apart from Philip there were two British officers who had been air-dropped: the first was Scottish Captain Davidson Sillitoe. He had already fought in Egypt. He was much loved and respected by his men, and was a very accomplished officer. The second, Captain André, was Welsh, young, and as he did not recognise danger, his courage seemed boundless!

HV: The people of Luzy and the whole area have great respect for all of you who came to fight alongside them.

KM: I also love the Morvan, and I go back often. I find such peace there, such deep peace, probably arising from these moments of grief and glory.

Grief and glory in 1944, when the maquisards, whatever their rank, their age, their religion, their profession and their political ideas, joined voluntarily, with no ulterior motives, in a common effort to free their Morvan.

I salute Captain Louis and all of our comrades who sacrificed their lives. The memory of each one of them is engraved in me forever.

Interview with Joseph Pinet

HV: Your Resistance group existed prior to the formation of the Louis Maquis. Where did you get your weapons from?

JP: We were supplied at the time through Switzerland. A certain "Poet" brought us the weapons. He came practically every week. I almost never saw him, because my wife received him. She alone knew the group's password, which changed every fortnight.

HV: So as to avoid, no doubt, any possibility of betrayal in case you were captured or tortured?

JP: Yes. At that time, there were only about thirty groups of Resistance fighters in France. And everything was planned so that in the event of one of us breaking down, the others would not be arrested. Obviously, it was not the same thing later on, especially towards the end, when the Maquis began to proliferate!

HV: There was indeed a large influx of maquisards during the last months of the war, of which I was one. You must grant me mitigating circumstances, because of my age! How did it start for you?

JP: I arrived in Luzy in 1941. I came from Laroche-Migennes in the Yonne, where I was Deputy Station Master. As I had been injured during the fighting in 1940 – three broken ribs and a perforated lung – I was often tired.

That's why I asked for a transfer to Luzy, to rest a little. It was in June 1941 that I was appointed Station Master.

HV: How old were you then?

JP: Fifty-three.

HV: I believe you are from the Luzy area?

JP: Yes. Like your father. I knew him well, we were even conscripts together. We went before the Review Board on 16 March 1909. It was the day of the trade fair, in Luzy, and there were, I remember, 20cm of snow!

HV: You have a good memory!

JP: In 1941, I rediscovered Luzy with pleasure. I stayed here quietly for a few months. There wasn't much rail traffic; sometimes three or four trainloads of German soldiers came for rest and recuperation in the area. But almost immediately, there was war in Russia; so, each week, convoys of several trains heading for the demarcation line went through. They carried a brigade or a division.

For 3 months, there were complicated manoeuvres. I constantly had to respond to German officers' demands. Being a station master was not easy!

Winter came. A butcher from the Jura, from Pagnay, made contact with me. He came to the area to buy cattle. How had he learned that I had had "problems" with the Germans in Laroche-Migennes, and been arrested and held for 3 days by the Gestapo?

HV: What had you done?

JP: I don't know if you remember, but the Germans sometimes opened mail. A person that I helped cross into the free zone wrote to me to thank me. Fortunately, my name had been misspelt: Pinay. I defended myself by saying: "That's not Pinet, n … e … t … It's someone who took a false name, at random. I have always respected the occupying army. I myself was in the occupying army in 1918 in Germany, and I never bothered your railway workers. I didn't think that you, Germans, would act differently in France!"

Thanks to a German station master who defended me, a charming man, by the way, I was able to leave the "red" cell where they had locked me up. Subsequently, it was difficult to carry on helping people escape, even with the assistance of the Sisters of Laroche-Migennes!

HV: You worked with nuns?

JP: Yes, with nuns; they were part of Abbot Kir's network, of which I was a member. But, as "Papa Klöch", the station master – that is how we had nicknamed him – had saved me from the Gestapo with great difficulty, I could no longer exercise my talents in the area.

HV: The Abbot Kir network was at that time only in charge of the "passages" into the free zone. It was not yet a true Resistance group, was it?

JP: No, because we had neither weapons nor ammunition.

HV: So, you were once again in contact with the Resistance by the winter of 1941?

JP: The winter of 1941/42 was terrible for the Germans; the trains coming
       from Russia were in dreadful condition. Often, horses died in the
       carriages, on the rye straw serving as their bedding, straw that measured
       almost 2m in length! Sometimes, the rye had even not been beaten.
       There were horses, but no artillery. It must have stayed somewhere near
       Smolensk!

So, I had met the butcher in Pagnay, who had learned my story concerning
Laroche-Migennes. I don't know who from. Perhaps from a railway worker,
you know how much they travel! He had approached me saying: "I know
you're a resistant. I myself am part of the Sochaux Group, a Peugeot factories'
group." He had openly named the Peugeot factories, and added: "You need
to come with us."
    "Tell me first what the purpose of your organisation is."
    "Blowing up trains with equipment we can get in Switzerland."
    "Ah, so it's serious."
    "Yes, it's very serious!"
So we agreed. He, like me, wanted contact with only one person.
The arrival of large equipment and explosives dates back to 1943, but as
early as 1941, we did get hold of some small equipment and a few firebombs
with the help of "Jules" Thomas.

HV: Who was supplying this equipment through Switzerland? The French
       or the British?
JP: I only know that it came from airdrops into Switzerland, where the
       French maquisards from the Jura entered with their weapons in their
       hands. The Maquis was very active in this border area. Packages of
       weapons arrived at the station addressed to Monsieur Perraudin in Luzy.

As there were about twenty Perraudins in the area, we had time to make all
the weapons disappear safely while the so-called recipient was sought. The
equipment was hidden either in a garage or in Larochemillay.
    One day, I received the order to blow up the track. This order came from
Captain "Henry", who had been a professor at the University of Oxford before
the war. I had spent a day with him in Besançon, so that he could show me
how to prepare explosives and detonators.
    He was dressed as a perfect Englishman. He "smelt" English from a distance
of 50m! He was supposedly suffering from tuberculosis and was being treated
in Besançon. It was obviously not true.
    Let me get back to my derailment. We had to go and collect a box of explos-
ives at Larochemillay, but I had no car. We couldn't ask just anyone, because
they needed commitment, and we couldn't afford the slightest indiscretion!

Finally, one of my men found one.

"Who is coming?"

"It's the butcher, Alphonse Perriault."

"Good. When will he meet us?"

"In half an hour."

Indeed, half an hour later, my Alphonse turns up and he asks me straight away: "So, where are we going?"

"To the woods at Velles."

HV: Was this your first attack?

JP: No, because we had already used the method of unbolting the rails, but this time it was our first attempt with plastic explosives, on 3 October 1943.

I remember it perfectly. We had hidden the plastic explosives and detonators under two pairs of chickens. If we had been stopped, the chickens might have been reassuring. And then we thought: "If they take our chickens, maybe they will be satisfied, and will possibly leave us the explosives!"

HV: When was your very first derailment?

JP: On 9 September 1942, at Rémilly. There were only three of us then.

So there we are, off to look for the crate with your cousin Alphonse. We get it out and open it up to take the plastic explosives out. I can still see the surprise on his face − "This is unbelievable, it's unbelievable … goodness, what a job!" − and he was stroking the grenades, stroking the revolvers and the machine guns. "I hope I'll get one."

"Yes, of course, we must wait for the Franche-Comté agent who is supposed to be coming!"

The one who was coming was known as Armand. He was a first-class saboteur, who spoke without ever unclenching his teeth. So we started the attacks, all over the place. Overall, 1943 went quite well.

However, we didn't do as much as we would have liked, because the tracks were very closely monitored. Several times, we received the order to "torpedo", and then we could not implement it. It was impossible!

HV: Where did the orders come from?

JP: Always from Franche-Comté. The train movements were reported to us: "Watch out, a train full of Tiger tanks is coming through." Once, we were asked to carry out sabotage on the Moulins line, between Paray-le-Monial and Digoin. It was on 11 October 1943, on a mail train. It was too far from Luzy, and too close to the demarcation line. We ran the risk of being arrested, not only during the sabotage, but also during the trip there or back.

On 2 December, there was another derailment. I had taught those in my group how to prepare the explosives and place the detonators so as to save the lives of the stoker and of the driver, who were generally French. To do this, we put the detonator 30m away from the load, and when the locomotive crushed it, it was the first carriage that blew up. We managed to spare the tender and the engine. We acquired, in time, a certain technique; derailments followed each other at a good pace, so that we successfully clocked up twenty-four of them.

HV: Twenty-four? That's quite something!

JP: We had some beauties! I remember one of them, at "kilometre 93". It was the anniversary of the Armistice: 11 November 1943. We managed to derail eleven of the sixteen carriages that made up the train.

HV: What kind of a train was it?

JP: A train full of German soldiers on leave. Number 800 and 931 trains crisscrossed France. They came from Karlsruhe, Düsseldorf or Kassel, and went towards the sun, to Biarritz generally.

HV: Were there many casualties?

JP: Yes. There was a lot of damage. On the other hand, during a derailment at the place known as Les Ardillys, the Germans got off quite lightly. We hadn't used plastic explosive in this particular attack. We had simply unbolted the rails. The locomotive remained standing, and ran between the two tracks, breaking everything over a distance of about 300m. Both tracks were completely crushed and ploughed up. I have never seen so much equipment broken as on that occasion.

HV: It was an excellent job!

JP: Yes, but there was just one broken arm among the German soldiers. There had not been a violent impact. We had a good laugh anyway, because we transferred a whole bunch of small "Gretchen" to the rescue train, which had been sent nearby. They were all wrapped in beautiful French fur coats, and we helped them to jump onto the ballast, because it was dark! There were at least 200 of them. They were all going to relieve teams of typists in Bordeaux, Biarritz and Rochefort.

It took at least 3 or 4 days to repair the tracks. In the first-aid equipment that had not been used, there were fifty stretchers. Knowing that we would perhaps need them one day, I hijacked them for the benefit of Luzy and Cercy-la-Tour Red Cross, hiding them under straw.

After the attack on 21 December, we observed a truce during Christmas and the New Year.

HV: I suppose that Armand was sometimes in the sector and helping you to prepare your derailments?

JP: Indeed. One day, on 5 January 1944, I met him at the station, and he asked me immediately: "Are you expecting a train of Tiger tanks?"

"Yes. There is a train of tanks expected, but I don't know if they are Tigers or Panthers! What do you want to do?"

"I would like to blow it up!"

"It's maybe not a good idea, because the head of the train is made up of carriages full of French passengers. There are four carriages with passengers; there may be Germans among them, but the French are certainly in vast majority: careful!"

"Do you have any powerful grenades?"

"Yes." Indeed, they were kept in a box of dressings on which I had put a seal to show that it was forbidden to open it.

We each took a grenade, and waited for the train to stop at the station. Armand said to me: "Let's throw one each under these machines!" I threw the first one, then Armand threw his. I realised that he had been seen by a German NCO who was in a carriage at the front of the train. I immediately ordered the train to be set in motion. The German became agitated and shouted to stop, but my employee, who did not understand German, and who had obeyed my order, thought he said to go faster. However, the German was yelling with all his strength: "Terrorists! Terrorists!" In any case, the train left quickly, which saved Armand.

When I met up with him afterwards, I said: "Watch out! A German NCO saw what you did, but I don't think he saw me." I thought that he would stop the train, and that the Gestapo from Étang would show up quickly. There was a Czech there, a real monster, of whom I was very wary. I would have preferred the Château-Chinon lot, who were much more easy-going Austrians.

As I had anticipated, the train was stopped at Étang for inspection, and the Gestapo arrived at Luzy.

Contrary to what I had thought, the NCO had seen two terrorists and approximately given my description. Fortunately, I wasn't wearing my cap! The Gestapo officer said to me: "One is tall, with a hat, and a black overcoat." That was me. "The other is smaller, stocky, dressed in khaki."

HV: Armand had escaped, meanwhile?
JP: Yes. He had.
HV: Did his grenade explode in the end?
JP: No. German bomb-disposal experts found it and defused it. My grenade did not explode either, but it wasn't discovered. Its detonator was perhaps out of order. Weapons and ammunition sometimes stopped over in Switzerland in somewhat damp cellars, and occasionally this caused problems.

As soon as the train left, Armand had in fact fled, and, before the arrival of the Gestapo, I had got seven crates of explosives and assorted weapons that were stored in the attic of the station transported to a safe place. I was expecting a thorough search.

Armand was now exposed, especially since he had been unwise enough to sign in under two different names when he stayed on two different occasions in the same hotel. From that moment on, he could no longer either stay in Luzy, or return there. I asked him to send someone from a network in Franche-Comté, because it was important for us to have a resistant unknown to the local rail track guards. There were sometimes missions that we couldn't undertake without being spotted immediately.

HV: You say that Armand was staying in a hotel, but he also slept at Passard's, didn't he?

JP: Yes, at Passard's and at the Hôtel de la Gare.

HV: He never stayed long, did he?

JP: He travelled a lot.

HV: The arrival of Louis as the head of the maquis must have also contributed to his moving away, mustn't it?

JP: Of course, but the business of the 5 January 1944 bombs was decisive.

Getting back to Louis, the Pagnay butcher, who was a big shot in the Franche-Comté Resistance, had said to me: "You're going to have a new captain," and he had then told me about his first contact with the young captain who had recently parachuted in.

He had just arrived at the butcher's house, and was standing in the dining room, when gendarmes came into the shop – the gendarmes came secretly, looking for meat – but as soon as he saw them, Louis jumped out of the window. When the butcher came to join him in the dining room, he found only his son, who said to him: "You know, the gentleman who was here just now, he left through the window."

HV: Louis, who had already experienced prison, certainly did not wish to go back.

JP: When he saw the police, he said to himself: "They're after me again. My cover has been blown."

HV: Let's put ourselves in his shoes. When you arrive in an unknown country, you might wonder about certain things. You met in Franche-Comté?

JP: Yes, near Pagnay.

HV: Did Louis know at that time that it was in the Luzy area that he was to set up his maquis?

JP: He knew. I said to him: "Everything is to be built up again from scratch, because our organisation is tired. You can no longer work with the local people, they've all been found out. We must bring in people from Franche-Comté." It was then that we got "Achilles", who had been permanently delegated by Armand. At the end of February, Achilles came, while two of our men were sent to Montchanin and Nevers.

The first thing Louis said to us was: "Careful, no recklessness, the main thing is to last." And then, towards the end of February: "We need to form groups." I was not in favour, because the Germans had decapitated the Autun and Chagny groups; the Gestapo was very well informed!

"We need to create a group in Étang," insisted Louis. "There are railway workers there, we must do something."

And I said: "We would do better to work with very small groups, and, if possible, with people who are not from round here."

Until June, we did nothing. It was at Les Fréchots that the maquis was being set up, with all the supply and airdrop issues.

HV: Although you stayed in Luzy, did you keep in touch with Louis and the maquis?

JP: I went up there every 2 or 3 days. As I remained in charge of the sabotage team and the village group in Luzy, we were connected directly by phone with the maquis, and we received our orders from Louis.

My sabotage team was made up of just four station officials, but I could also tap into the Luzy town group.

Meanwhile, your cousin Alphonse had fallen ill, but he continued to lend us his car; two or three times, we borrowed it to pick up the wounded of the Louis Maquis, or other maquis. That's how we saved three or four maquisards of the Socrates Group. Then we camouflaged them to get them treated at the Château de Magny.

HV: In June 1944, was the activity intense?

JP: Hugely! We had to work twice as hard, as far as the attacks were concerned. We were helped by the RAF because the Louis Maquis was not like the others. It could request support from the RAF by radio, and get airdrops quickly, while others could wait for weeks. We armed some in Saône-et-Loire and in Bas-Morvan.

HV: In June, July and August, sabotages were numerous and the famous story of the crane was just one of the daily exploits!

JP: It was 10 August, a failed exploit. It was blown up, oh yes! But we should never have demolished it; we needed to keep it. I had said:."Just blow up a cog!" However, the NCO set a load of 30kg of plastic explosive. He broke it, destroyed it completely! We felt that it was the end, that we needed to try and save equipment, and not completely destroy either the Vierzon crane, or the 50-ton crane.

HV: Obviously, it was tempting to destroy everything.

JP: Yes, it was tempting, it felt good!

The same non-commissioned officer torched a petrol tanker near Larochemillay, rather than keeping the petrol for the maquis. Sometimes, in the heat of the action, we overdid it, or we became reckless. Some young maquisards were killed because they ignored basic safety rules.

HV: I have found in the maquis diary that, at the beginning, you used modified 75mm shells for your derailments.

JP: That was before we got equipment from Switzerland. M., a maquisard from the early days and a former non-commissioned artillery officer, had modified the detonators to incorporate a booby-trap, but this was not exceptional.

It was less exceptional than how he fooled the Gestapo, narrowly escaping from them every time. It seemed as though he could smell them coming!

HV: And you yourself, how did you manage to pull the wool over the Gestapo's eyes, since the many derailments caused investigations? You had already been a suspect in Laroche-Migennes. So did the Germans not have the bright idea of putting two and two together, and questioning a certain Monsieur Pinet a little more closely?

JP: I had to answer their questions when they came into the station, so I talked, I talked a lot. They had to be stopped from pursuing their enquiry. I didn't hide that there was Resistance in the area, and I added: "We haven't invented anything; you did this before us in 1812–13, when you harassed Napoleon's armies! Look," – I was showing them the map of the railways – "attack near Luzy, attack on the Corbigny line. Yet another near Épinac; the whole Morvan region is in the hands of the Maquis! And what can we do, in the stations? They don't need us, to derail trains!"

HV: So you were never arrested again?

JP: Yes, I was, on 11 August, after the bombing of the crane; they kept me all afternoon. Once more, it was a German officer, a "two stripe lieutenant", a pastor, who released me against the advice of an SS railwayman, who was not inclined to spare me.

HV: Did you get any help from the population of Luzy? Your activity must eventually have been known there.

JP: The population always supported and assisted us, as much with supplies to the Louis Maquis, as with information they could give us.

I was chairman of the Committee for the Liberation of Luzy, and I can tell you that I did not have to take a single sanction against any of its inhabitants.

HV: So it was much calmer than in some other cities in the Nièvre?

JP: Yes. Two or three people were shaved, wrongly. The Maquis took some prisoners, Petainists, but these people were not pro-German! It was regrettable, just like the trouble that the station master at M. [name omitted] had, because his kid had drawn swastikas on his school book! But all this, it must be repeated, did not get very far and, overall, the Liberation went very well. You know as well as I do that the Resistance in France, by its sacrifices and its abuses, made history. And I do mean, by its sacrifices and its abuses!

You must remember that we no longer had either police or gendarmes. Here, we had created a Committee for the Defence of the Population. But elsewhere?

HV: The gendarmes were with the Maquis. They formed the 6th or the 7th Company.

JP: Oh yes, but some were old, sick. I remember. We went looking for digitalis to treat some of them; they also caught bronchitis! They were full of goodwill, but a little too old to make perfect maquisards! Most of them were war gendarmes, "reservists".

HV: Did you know, in 1944, that Louis was French?

JP: Yes, we knew; we also knew that he was working with the British, and right at the beginning, we were told: "Watch out, he belongs to the 'Intelligence Service'; don't contact him."

HV: Oh really, and why?

JP: I don't know, exactly. It was Major Roche, Major "Moreau" at the time, who had received these orders, and had sent them to us from Saint-Honoré-les-Bains.

HV: Was this to prevent the British from setting up a maquis in the Morvan?

JP: Why? I did wonder. Anyway it didn't last, because eventually Louis and Moreau met and got along very well! Louis even obtained, at the request of Major Moreau, airdrops for other maquis in the Nivernais.

HV: On the other hand, it is hard to imagine that you were able to lead a normal life. You must have been constantly tense, at the ready. You lived daily alongside Germans who fought with shadows, and were looking for any hint, any opportunity to arrest the one or several culprits. Twenty-four derailments, you must admit that they had reasons to be nervous!

JP: Not to mention the other tricks that we also played on them! The "labels" trick must have made them suffer too! When a carriage apparently containing important equipment passed through Luzy, if it were bound for Strasbourg, for example, we removed the label, and put another one on for Lyon or Nantes instead. At the same time, we asked the engine driver for the bill of lading so that we could check it, and later on he was given another one in exchange, which was perfectly compatible with the new destination. I had a fine selection of labels and bills that I had collected from other stations.

This is why there were a number of carriages full of spare parts, wandering around for a long time before finding their proper destination.

It must have damaged the Germans, and it was easy to do!

HV: By the way, did you ever "lift" materials as supplies for the Maquis?

JP: Indeed, several carriages of wood for gas generators were unloaded for maquisards' trucks. Meanwhile, four carriages of coal went to Luzy schools and to the blacksmiths. Another time, a carriage of 20 tonnes of manganese was tipped onto the embankment. It came from Spain – Bilbao – and was going to Essen to make steel for artillery manufacture.

HV: It was efficient and almost "peaceful"!

JP: Yes, but we were involved in tougher actions. In 1942/43, trains carried many horse-drawn artillery regiments going on leave. They had stored oats for their horses in Luzy Station. "Jules" opened the bags and added handfuls of small nails. So the regiments were immobilised.

HV: How did you think this up?

JP: The recipe was German! They had applied it to our occupation army.

HV: Now tell me about the engine drivers. They can't have enjoyed crossing the Morvan! They needed a fair bit of courage.

JP: During a derailment caused by Armand, carriages were on their sides from bank to bank, and on that occasion, the engine had not been saved because the coupling had broken at the moment of the explosion. When I arrived with the rescue squad, we were initially greeted by "travellers", fairly unfriendly gentlemen of the Kriegsmarine [the German Navy], then beside the engine, now upside down on the ballast, by the driver and his stoker. It was the same engine driver as on a previous derailment. He cried out: "They'll kill us in the end!"

Without doubt, the first time at Les Ardillys, when the two tracks had been destroyed over several hundred metres, the train driver can't have had much fun either, and on that occasion he was lucky not to have been killed or badly scalded by the steam. I couldn't explain to him that, according to our practice, we had put the detonator 30m from the bomb, to try and spare him!

HV: What damage did the explosive cause?

JP: The rail was usually shattered over 3–4m.

By the KING'S Order the name of

Monsieur Joseph-Marie Pinet,

was placed on record on

26 November, 1946,

as commended for brave conduct.
I am charged to express His Majesty's
high appreciation of the service rendered.

C. R. Attlee

Prime Minister and First Lord
of the Treasury

Joseph-Marie Pinet, railway stationmaster in Luzy, receives on 26 November 1946 a significant honour "By the King's Order", in recognition of his actions, including the derailment of twenty-four German trains loaded with equipment and soldiers. Joseph Pinet joined the Resistance as early as 1941. He first belonged to the resistance group in Luzy, then in late 1943, after the founding of the Louis Maquis, he worked directly with Captain Louis.

HV: Did it take much explosive?

JP: About 1 lb, not more, but we used two detonators, for reliability. Once, in Sémelay, we used two detonators, but it was raining; so, the explosive didn't go off. Afterwards, we had to go back, to retrieve everything! It wasn't a very pleasant job. Fortunately, at other times, we had the opportunity to laugh a little.

HV: Yes, so do you have an amusing anecdote to finish on?

JP: There were quite a few! Do you want the one about the Winchester rifles?

HV: Let's go for the Winchester rifles story!

JP: On the occasion of one of the first airdrops, a dozen Winchester rifles arrived. They were real gems. As soon as the container was unpacked, there were only five left! They were handed out: one for a section leader, one to old Jules – in short, to the crack shots.

At that time, the maquis was still at La Croix de Meu, and the men had attacked a German truck, killing the driver, and brought the truck back to Louis, very pleased with themselves. But Louis, who did not want to be spotted, ordered them to drive it away from the camp, and burn it.

Upon their return, he added: "You made a mistake attacking a truck near the camp. We now have to stand guard on the four roads leading here: the road to Mont Beuvray, the one coming from Poil and the other two, and put out patrols."

On the road to Mont Beuvray, there was Jules, with three other men, and the only weapons they had were two Winchester rifles. But they no longer had a single cartridge between them.

So Jules called one of his men: "Go back to the guardhouse, down to the cellar, and you will find a box of cartridges there."

The man left. Later in the night, Jules heard an indistinct noise, a German, maybe. He shouted: "Halt! Stop right there!" The noise continued softly. "Stop or I'll shoot!" Still no response. "I'm shooting!" Then a voice replied, quietly: "What with, you clown! I'm bringing you the cartridges!"

The German Debacle:
Diary of a Luzy Resident

Reliving, in thought, these "hot" months of the summer of 1944, I had to admit that, isolated in my maquis, or sent on the "wrong" roads looking for an enemy I could never catch nor fight, I had not fully assessed the often tragic or indeed grotesque scenario of the German debacle, while others, civilians from the Route Nationale 73, had rubbed shoulders every day with retreating soldiers!

When I discovered the diary of a Luzy resident, I became acquainted with the detail of these terrible times. The diary (an excerpt from which is given below) was written by Madame Forneret and hidden between the top of a wooden kitchen table and its drawer during the retreat of the German troops.

Thursday, 10 August 1944

For a few days, we have been witnessing the debacle of the German troops. At the station, the Resistance blew up a crane. The railway track is now impassable towards Étang, and will no doubt be difficult to repair.

The *Kommandantur* immediately investigated in Luzy and around Millay and Larochemillay, where a farm was burned down in retaliation. Eight men were arrested and taken to Moulins-sur-Allier.

11 August

My house was searched from top to bottom by four German soldiers.

15 August

The Germans released six of their eight prisoners on Sunday, but they had to return from Moulins under their own steam because regular public transport is now non-existent. We see trucks loaded with troops going by. The "removal" has really begun.

17 August

Luzy is due to burn! Fortunately, the Germans are ordered to leave immediately for Autun. A Resistance van has been attacked, a sergeant killed and two maquisards wounded. The sergeant was buried in Luzy at 4 p.m., accompanied only by the village policeman and two pallbearers.

18 August

Several enemy convoys came through Luzy today. The last one, consisting of artillery and ammunition trucks, was attacked at La Goulette. We heard shots all night.

19 August

In the morning, two buses of Germans return to Luzy by road from Autun. People are frightened, men hide. Soldiers steal a truck to take their survivors. They go and find the mayor. Doctor Dollet and his son are taken as hostages. The German Army, which is retreating, passes through ceaselessly until the curfew, which has been established at 9.30 p.m. For two days, convoys have been staying on the promenade and the fairground.

Sunday, 20 August

Since 7.30 this morning, in the rain, there has been a procession of trucks, cars (mainly Citroën), artillery and soldiers. We even saw women this afternoon. It is said to be the Polish Embassy in Vichy, fleeing to the East.

We've noticed vehicles from all areas, a disparate bunch, with suitcases, mattresses, blankets, carpets, etc. Almost all the trucks are carrying spare bicycles, not to mention bags of wheat and potatoes, poultry and even pigs! Towards evening, the Japanese diplomatic corps came through Luzy.

21 August

As early as 6.30 a.m., passage of troops, followed by a Red Cross convoy. There are many cars from the Allier department. At 3 p.m., three motorcycles and a large and beautiful car, an RM 6, park on the side of the road. Apparently, it's Marshal Pétain! Others follow, and then more cars from the Allier, with many women among the soldiers. Until the evening, it is a continuous stream of troops and artillery transport. Two Tiger tanks go by among trucks from the Gironde and Vienne departments.

A column of vehicles has been bombed on the road, beyond the oil processing factory. I was afraid, because I happened to be going to get my milk at Madame L.'s with Annie, when a plane appeared. The Germans immediately took up firing positions, very close to us. We then heard shots for nearly an hour. Monsieur R. told me that a German casualty was taken to the pharmacy, where Dr B. took a bullet out of him. A German NCO said that two officers, a young one and an old one, were killed 25km from here. We learn that a truck is blocking the road and two farms are burning. The damaged German equipment is torched. We believe that this is Resistance activity.

We now have thunderstorms, which cut off the electricity supply. In the evening, we are tired; nerves are tense. Finally, the night was pretty quiet and we could rest.

22 August

About 10 o'clock, the cavalcade restarts. Useless trucks are destroyed and replaced by vehicles requisitioned locally. This is how Madame P.'s truck and driver, a 68-year-old man, leave with the troops.

At midday, a convoy stops for lunch; they go and fetch drink at the well where J. G. is drawing water, but fill their containers with cognac, to which they add lumps of sugar. The troops have been bombed twice by plane. Yesterday, Monsieur D. and his son-in-law were killed by the Germans at Fontaine-Alène. They were only running to extinguish the fire that soldiers had lit in one of the haystacks on their farm.

We are tired of this procession; fortunately, they announced on the radio that the Americans are in Montargis. We had bread for the first time without ration cards.

23 August

Vichy militiamen go by with their wives and their children. Rumour has it that Paris has been liberated.

24 August

I get a letter, which has been brought from Paris on a bicycle. It dates back to the 18th, therefore before the battle; I am worried.

German troops continue to pass by, even by bike or on horseback. A munitions truck blows up near the road to Fours. Some militiamen are still circulating. We learn that Romania has asked for an armistice, and that Bulgaria might be following suit!

25 August

We heard a lot of planes last night. At 8 o'clock, we see large numbers of German troops. Maybe they are intending to regroup. They are still an impressive force, but we have to hope that they can't do anything. Then we witness the arrival of members of the Vichy militia.

On our doorstep two of them take aim at the driver of a car who wants to overtake a truck. He gets through anyway.

It is the cavalry now; horses are very beautiful, much more beautiful than men!

26 August

I wake up at 7 o'clock, with gunshots over towards Nevers. Seven trucks of Germans armed to the teeth are quickly sent as reinforcements. An hour later, everything seems finished, and the convoy proceeds to Autun. At 11 o'clock, two German soldiers pass by on bicycles looking ridiculous. The storm breaks out, with very heavy rain.

27 August

They are saying that the bridge over the Selle River, a few kilometres before Autun, has been blown up. We've had no electricity since yesterday, so no radio either. Around 7 p.m., a convoy goes through Luzy, then a little later thirty trucks stop, with troops and guns, as well as men on foot or in horse-drawn carts. They sleep in the community hall.

29 August

Procession of Germans and militiamen. About 8 o'clock, two farms are burned in Bussières, one belonging to Monsieur H. and the other to the town of Semur. One thousand two hundred men, with their 700 horses, are staying in Luzy. Field guns are camouflaged in Saint-André. At night, we can hear the cavalry. Germans go about on bicycles. We see troops moving about at night for the first time. We had electricity back from 1 o'clock till 7 o'clock in the morning.

30 August

The people of Luzy have been told by the village policeman with his drum that a German officer was killed in La Vernière – no details are given – and that the area is threatened with reprisals if the slightest incident occurs.

Troops are still retreating. Around 8 o'clock in the evening, a regiment of young soldiers stops. They drink cognac and Grand Marnier straight from the bottle, probably to lift their spirits.

Artillery is in town, and plans to spend the night here.

Field guns are everywhere, ready to fire.

31 August

Night of terror: at midnight, artillery fire and gunfire. About 6 o'clock, German soldiers flee on foot or on bicycles, in the storm that has just burst.

When the last soldiers have left Luzy, I go back upstairs to bed, and sleep until 9.30. I am then awakened by further troops.

They say that there is fighting in Châlons-sur-Marne, and that in the Rhone Valley, "they" are in Valence.

1 September

Fortunately, one night quiet!

A lone plane flies over Luzy three times.[10] In the centre of the town, soldiers stay with locals. Madame C. is putting eight of them up.

We still have no electricity for a large part of the day.

2 September

No transport is possible, even on a bicycle, because it would immediately be stolen!

The passage of German troops now runs continuously. Around noon, a Citroën stops. An officer asks me for water, and has our stable opened up. Then, another one steps out; he wears three gold stars on his shoulder. Is he a lieutenant colonel? He speaks perfect French. Women greet him. He goes into the workshop to wash. After a meticulous wash, he speaks to me and tells me that for 3 months, he has not heard from his family, that he is from Berlin, and that he saw his house burn down during his last leave. Another soldier comes to wash his hands.

These are officers from the *Kommandantur* in La Rochelle.

3 September

As I feared, the night was more than hectic. All night long, convoys of big guns crossed the city noisily. The Germans take everything as they pass through:

---

[10]There were, in fact, three Lancaster bombers, which parachuted weapons at different intervals to the Louis Maquis for its operation known as "Leon is dreaming of dancing the beguine".

they steal my wood, they pinch my tomatoes and my fruit. These are starving and sleep-deprived people, who occasionally stop for a moment.

We are not going to mass.

When an aeroplane flies over us, all the equipment is immediately hidden under the trees and the men come and take refuge around our houses.

Airforce officers, accompanied by a woman, speak to us as they go through, and admit that it really is a retreat.

I can listen to the radio, electricity came back on last night. But how long for?

The Allies are supposedly 70km beyond Brussels, in Sedan and Longwy. Paratroopers have apparently been dropped on Belfort. Are the German armies therefore surrounded? The soldiers, who are too tired to carry on walking, have "borrowed" horses and carts from farms, with farmers to drive them. Many of these hapless farmers are from the Berry region.

Here, requisitions have started. After the theft of cars, trucks and bikes, it's now horses and carts.

An officer listens to the radio at J. G.'s. He is dismayed to learn that the Allies have crossed the Belgian border.

Ambulance convoys go by; they are no longer armed as they were at the beginning. It's an increasingly ill-assorted procession, which goes on all night long.

Soldiers go into the gardens, and take fruit and vegetables; they are tired and hungry. J. G. has his barn and his attic filled with troops. A subaltern comes to my house looking for a room for his officer.

The town is full of men and equipment; the radio announces that all roads in the Nièvre have been mined by the Maquis.

4 September

We are awoken by an explosion at 7.30. Is this the departure of the troops? I go down in great haste. Two planes fly over Luzy at low altitude. Soldiers abandon two crates of grenades in the ditch near the house as they flee. J. G. finds three crates outside his door. There are bullets and ammunition lying around everywhere.

The tanks are still in Rue de Trezillon. Yesterday, I was told that they had no fuel.

A 17-year-old young man was shot at Madam C.'s at Montreuillon. The Germans reportedly found incriminating papers on him.

A barricade had been prepared on the road to Toulon, quite far from here, and a lost convoy fell into the ambush. This young man, who was taken close by, was almost hanged by his feet from a tree. Finally, the German officer commanding the detachment gave in, and he had him shot. The nearest farm in Auzon was burned down.

5 September

At 2 o'clock in the afternoon, four fighter planes dive on Luzy, and spray us with bullets; to hide, two Germans force entry into the kitchen, where we are.

Last night, Hindus stayed in town and spread terror among women; twice, they came here, once to ask for bread, but especially to see if there weren't any girls; later, to search for bicycles. While they're about it, they go through the house; but my bicycle is well hidden in the attic.

These Hindu soldiers are so enterprising that women and girls on their own spend the night with neighbours where they know they will be protected; but, on the road to Autun, several men were almost shot, because these Hindus wanted "young ladies" at all cost.

German officers had actually warned us: "Tell women not to go out, and beware of rapists!"

We are living through days of terror: we women all sleep in the same room.

The radio tells us that the Allies are on the Rhine, and that Belgium and Holland are partly liberated.

6 September

Again and again, disparate bunches of troops go past. They sometimes stop for an hour or two at our door. The garden and the fruit trees are now completely stripped bare.

This morning, we saw a large convoy of trucks camouflaged with olive branches.

As I go down to prepare lunch, a German falls under a truck. His back is broken; we hoist him onto a truck, and they are gone without further ado. This is a boy who is not more than 17 years old!

J. G. tells me that two Allied armies have met up in a town in central France. The Swiss radio announced it, at 8 o'clock this morning.

We have the impression that the majority of Germans don't care about being taken prisoner; what a shambles! They take everything from us: bread, fodder, potatoes, meat and horses in the fields.

A farmer who had been requisitioned, and had left from the vicinity of Bourges last night with his three horses and his cart, was able to talk to us for a few moments; his brother-in-law, who was requisitioned at the same time, is a little further down the road; they are exhausted, men and horses!

Since Bourges, they have only stopped for an hour to sleep. He has seen eight horses fall down from exhaustion; the Germans finished them off immediately, no doubt so we would have nothing left!

J. G. saw another driver coming from Angers. Do the Germans think that in this way they will avoid the machine-gunning of their convoys?

We learn that the Allies are in Cluny and Sennecy-le-Grand. I wonder when this pitiful exodus will be over.

Our bread is taken to a house nearby where we can pick it up, because we are afraid to go into town and leave our house open to looting.

7 September

Night of horror and nightmare. We women sleep on our beds in our clothes, and leave our inner connecting door open so as to be closer to our neighbours!

My cellar has been completely ransacked; there is nothing left! It is definitely an army of stragglers and looters! They took my last rabbit, and forced the door of our stable. I don't know exactly what they took. We are physically and emotionally exhausted by the passage of these troops. Last night, four young girls were raped.

The Germans were attacked for 2 hours late this afternoon.

8 September

Wounded Frenchmen have been finished off by the Germans, on the pretence that they were terrorists. Ten died; the rest of the German column, attacked and exhausted, is trailing miserably behind; many lean on sticks as they go up the road to Autun; two of them come and sit for a few moments on the bench behind the house.

We had a better night. I feel less disconsolate. I do not dwell on the looting of the cellar, saying to myself that one must not attach importance to this kind of thing.

Some troops are still straggling along, but few.

A peasant and a driver are on their way back from Beaune. The peasant has left his two teams of horses behind. He is from Bourges, and the driver is from Bordeaux; the latter abandoned his truck, strafed and unusable. Americans are rumoured to be in Étang, Fours and Toulon. This morning, we could hear the field guns, but since 10 o'clock, everything has been quiet.

Two or three columns, including cavalry, still travel through.

9 September

This morning, there has been fighting near Fours, but Luzy seems calmer. I take this opportunity to do a little shopping, because I haven't been able to for over a week.

As I get to the town centre, an FFI car appears. What a surprise! With their revolvers at the ready, they rush to the Town Hall; others arrive, as well as marines from Vichy; they leave immediately in the direction of Fours.

No Germans have travelled through today. There were only two planes, which flew over the road skimming the houses; tonight, we hear some field guns. There must be fighting in La Comelle.

We have electricity! The radio announces that Le Creusot, Autun, Beaune, Châlons and Chagny have been freed. The men have received the order to prepare quarters for the maquisards.

10 September

At dawn, I hear rustling in the grass. Through the window, I see fifteen Germans walking in single file, rifles at the ready.

When I get up, everyone living on the Autun road is talking about it. The Maquis are told. An hour later, FFI are sent to La Comelle, and now there is fierce fighting there.

We have been hearing gunfire in every direction since this morning.

Four British aircraft fly over and once again bomb what we assume to be the Autun road; it seems as though it's in Bussières, it seems so close!

At 11.30, 800 young FFIs go on parade and raise a flag on the Town Hall; then war veterans meet; the day is more cheerful than last Sunday, but we feel that it is not over yet; field guns still thunder.

At last, Issy-l'Évêque, Étang, are liberated and we are too, but Germans are still sighted all over the place, in small groups; the young maquisards who are here chase them; they will not leave until tomorrow morning.

This morning, we went to see the parade, which was followed by a wine reception at the Town Hall. I am sorry not to have a decent bottle to share with France and Roger.

A German deserter and a Frenchwoman have been arrested; they were going down the road to Autun in a tipcart.

11 September

I had not slept so well for a long time!

FFIs settle in Luzy, but many are sent as reinforcements to the Decize area; seventy-two were taken prisoner round here today; yesterday, near la Commelle, 400 Germans surrendered.

We hear that Saint-Symphorien-de-Marmagne, and part of Mesvres were burnt down by the Germans; we also hear about the destruction of part of the factory at Le Creusot.

12 September

British aircraft fly overhead with airdrops for the Maquis.

All kinds of people are travelling on the roads. Many are farmers or drivers requisitioned by the Germans, who are returning home on foot; two of them, who have come from Dijon, tell us that the town has most probably been liberated.

The Americans arrived in Luzy this evening, where they will spend the night, having come from Saint-Honoré-les-Bains. We have been waiting for their arrival for months!

An American column is in Luzy, and is leaving this morning. The FFIs are cleaning up the area, and taking a few prisoners, but now they are mostly bringing back abandoned German equipment.

My three Parisians arrive by car; at last, we have been reunited!

Part III: Forms of Resistance

The Role of the Resistance in the Liberation of France

With the passing of years, we can better know, and therefore understand, the respective roles played in the liberation of France by the first French resistants, of various affiliations; General de Gaulle's Free French, operating from London; and the Special Operations Executive (SOE) created by Sir Winston Churchill to assist the Resistance throughout those parts of Europe occupied by the Germans (the French branch was headed by Colonel Maurice Buckmaster).

The organisation of the first Resistance and intelligence networks on French soil began almost as soon as the armistice was signed. Six months after the cessation of hostilities, forty-eight networks had already been created. The increase was constant thereafter before reaching its peak in 1944.

From June to November 1940, during the terrible Battle of Britain, the British only had access to information provided by the French because they had no intelligence networks on the ground. But it was essential for the Royal Air Force to know what was happening on the airfields of the Luftwaffe, the departures of aircraft, the numbers and types of planes. This allowed the British to predict, and therefore to counter with a maximum of efficiency, the many bombings that Britain was then enduring. At that time, when one could expect a German landing on the British coast, the situation was critical. The Germans had air supremacy with 1,000 fighter planes, 400 Stukas and 1,200 bombers, whereas the British side could only muster 600 fighters. So, they needed to have the best information possible, to be used to maximum effect. This was the case, thanks to the intelligence networks of the Resistance which were already in place, and it is fair to say that they played a very significant part in the final victory of this gigantic battle in the skies.

At the beginning, the first Resistance fighters had no communication with Free France, which had taken refuge in Britain. Henri Fresnay made it clear: "Without any links with London, with only our own resources, we recruited our executives, devised our organisations, invented our methods, completed the hard apprenticeship of clandestine life. What were we obeying if not the call of our consciences? We had no contact with de Gaulle and no one, apart from the odd exception, had heard the call of 18 June." It is really from 1943 onwards that Fighting France (as it was now known) put a lot of effort into increasing its help to the Resistance, providing money and weapons from London.

In 4 years, the Resistance became an important and well-organised force. At the time of the Normandy landings, it was a real army ready for battle. According to Jacques Canaud: "The overall figure of maquisards that we can retain for all the Maquis in summer 1944, is of the order of 300,000 men, divided into a thousand maquis". General Eisenhower wrote in *Crusade in Europe*, his memoirs: "It is estimated that in our campaign the FFI (French Forces of the Interior) represented in numbers the equivalent of 15 divisions. The great support they gave us by enabling us to cross France at speed confirmed this fact."

However, maintaining unity of command, therefore of actions, under the aegis of the National Resistance Council (*Conseil National de la Résistance* – CNR) was not easy. The creation of the CNR was, at the time, seen by many in the Resistance as a kind of stranglehold of politicians over fighters, and a return of the old parties that had led France to disaster. Resistance fighters, for the most part, "dreamed" of new politics, made by new people.

To answer Churchill who had said to de Gaulle, "You say you are France. You're not France, you are Fighting France," the latter was to politicise the Resistance, to prove to both Americans and British that there was a real resurrection of the French State. To do that he could only rely on the old parties because at least they existed, but at the same time he exposed himself to comments from the resistants who thought, like Brossolette: "You are pulling skeletons out of the closet." De Gaulle was to "pay for it" on 20 January 1946. Leaving power, he stated: "The party system has reappeared. I disapprove." But could he, at the time, have done otherwise?

The recognition of de Gaulle by the Allies had therefore been difficult, and it took all the General's tenacity to earn it.

President Roosevelt, after the armistice, thought that France was a finished country! Had he not said on 2 July 1943 to General Giraud visiting Washington: "France no longer exists!"? At the same time, he informed General Eisenhower: "Immediately after the landing, France will be considered occupied territory, a currency minted in the United States will have full face value and an administration called AMGOT (Allied Military Government Occupied Territory) will replace the French public employees working in the country."

For his part, Anthony Eden recounts in his memoirs that Roosevelt was speaking of the possible creation "of a state called Wallonia, which would include the Walloon part of Belgium, Luxembourg, Alsace-Lorraine and a part of Northern France."

We can see the consideration which de Gaulle enjoyed at that time, especially since in London, Winston Churchill really did not help matters by writing to Anthony Eden: "I ask my colleagues to consider as a priority the question of whether we should eliminate de Gaulle as a political force as a matter of urgency. If this were the case, we would say to the French National Committee that we shall cease to communicate with it or give it money, as long as de Gaulle is part of the Committee ... For my part, I shall be more than willing to defend this policy in Parliament and to show everyone that the movement of Resistance in France, which is at the heart of the Gaullist ideology, can no longer be.identified with this vain and malicious man." This is what was written on 21 May 1943 about the leader of Fighting France!

Fortunately, de Gaulle had "felt" for a long time that it was necessary that all the Resistance in France be grouped around a single man: himself. So Jean Moulin did that job, uniting under the banner of the French Forces of the Interior (FFI), in February 1942, the Secret Army (*Armée Secrète* − AS), the FTPs (*Francs-Tireurs et Partisans*) of communist obedience and various other Resistance movements.

Roosevelt and Churchill had been challenged. De Gaulle, whom the CNR, in Algiers, had already managed to set up as the head of the provisional government, could now enable France to avoid the military administration which would have been imposed by the Allies. In this way, Roosevelt had to admit that France "existed" again!

Although the Resistance was active throughout the war, an extraordinary development of its activity took place from the moment of the landings on the Normandy beaches. Looking back, all observers agreed that the German divisions had been delayed and weakened thanks to the activity of the FFI. This enabled the Allies to hold on to the landing sites, before undertaking a more rapid progression through France. Albert Chambon in his remarkable work *When France was Occupied* thinks that "whilst it is clear that the Allies would have eventually beaten Germany anyway with or without the Resistance, it is no less true that without it, there was every chance that the landings would have failed in June 1944 and that the liberation of Europe would have been delayed for who knows how many months." Chambon goes on to explain that the top three German armoured divisions of the Waffen-SS were at the time held further south, up to 700km from the landing beaches, by significant retaliatory actions against the Maquis.

What worried Eisenhower most was D-Day+3, with the supposed arrival, according to the Allied strategists, of relief SS armoured divisions. Fortunately, according to Chambon, "The assigned objective, Resistance, was fulfilled, since those much-vaunted divisions arrived on the battlefield in a state of disarray and with a delay that proved fatal for the Reich." Moreover, Churchill says in his memoirs: "The movement of the French Resistance, which was 30,000 men strong in the region, played an important role, and thanks to it Brittany was quickly liberated." The concerted actions of the FFI enabled Patton, secured from the rear, to head at speed towards the Loire and the Seine. It is estimated that the Resistance contained, at this decisive moment in the landing battles, the equivalent of six German divisions and took 20,000 prisoners.

The Triad of the SOE, Resistance and FFI

The relationship between the SOE and Free French Forces was not always easy because General de Gaulle wanted to represent the whole of the Resistance movement on French soil. He also wanted recognition from the Allies, but at first they did not consider him sufficiently significant – especially Roosevelt, who was more inclined to turn towards Vichy and Admiral Darlan; and who, in Morocco and Algeria, had not immediately acknowledged the "sovereignty" of de Gaulle, favouring General Giraud over him for a while.

Whilst at the top in London there were differences of opinion between nations, on the ground Jean Moulin and André Dewavrin ("Colonel Passy") from FFI were fortunately able to co-operate with the French section of SOE.

In France the Maquis, whatever their political persuasion, soon had only one objective: defeating the enemy. Jean Moulin, who arrived in London in September 1941, was immediately to be given by de Gaulle the role of unifying the resistants on French soil, whether on the right or on the left, into a single force. Parachuted into France on 31 December 1941, he created his first Co-ordinating Committee on 27 November 1942.

The FFI (French Forces of the Interior) were thereafter able to gather all the maquis together in a single movement for the liberation of French soil.

I will cite only one example of this understanding. In August 1944, when I was in the Louis Maquis, a fierce battle began 50km to the west of the Morvan. In considerable numbers, the Germans attacked two maquis which were quite close to each other and had set themselves up in farms on the edge of a vast forest. The Mariaux Maquis was 550 men strong and the Julien Maquis had 263 men. The German attack had been preceded by numerous air raids on the maquis positions. The 4,500 German soldiers took the farms with difficulty before the maquis dispersed through the forest.

At this point, the head of the Nièvre FFI asked certain maquis to intervene. Three came from the Morvan and a total of seven countered the German attack.

After 5 days of heavy fighting, the Germans were unable to prevent the maquisards from withdrawing in an orderly manner to the maquis of the Morvan. The Wehrmacht had failed. It returned to its barracks in Nevers, taking with it more than 300 dead and 1,000 injured soldiers. As for the Mariaux and Julien maquisards, they had lost thirty-one of their own. Attacking them in the forest was no easy task!

This difficult battle had proved three things: that different maquis were able to join forces; that the armament they had, thanks to further airdrops requested by the SOE, was sufficient to face well-organised German forces; and finally that the maquisards were very good fighters.

The Germans learned their lesson and refrained from attacking the Louis Maquis, which they assumed too powerful and strongly entrenched in its Morvan woods.

Without airdrops secured through the SOE, the French Resistance could never have assumed the huge part it played in the liberation of our country.

Over 10,500 tons of weapons, ammunition and other supplies were airdropped to all of the maquis, especially after the Normandy landings, over the course of 7,498 sorties by Allied planes.

The 1,784 SOE agents, trained in Britain, including many Frenchmen such as Captain Louis, organised or helped the maquis by making the delivery of weapons possible. The first three SOE agents were parachuted into France in May 1941.

Women were not absent from the SOE. Fifty fought on French soil, and they accomplished the same difficult work as the men. Thirteen were killed in battle or executed by the Germans.

It is thanks to the SOE in Franche-Comté that the first resistants in the Morvan were able to derail German trains near Luzy, on 9 September 1942, including those of soldiers on leave who were returning mainly from the Eastern Front to go and rest on the French coasts. Joseph Pinet, Luzy's station master, derailed twenty-four trains with his team. After the war, he was decorated "By the King's Order" by Prime Minister Clement Attlee.

We can see clearly that the operational merger of Colonel Buckmaster's British SOE with the Resistance hastened the achievement of final victory.

There actually were, after General de Gaulle's return to France, a few SOE members expelled, but it was more a matter of "personal settlements".

The Louis Maquis

Now that we have acquired better information over the years, we must clarify how this important maquis of 1,901 men was able to live and fight the enemy, while remaining hidden in the Morvan's forests and its small villages.

The four earlier interviews of Captain Baptist, Abbot Bonin, Émile Passard and the Luzy station master Joseph Pinet have given an idea of the difficulties encountered in the setting up of the maquis.

The publication by Jacques Canaud entitled *The Morvan Maquis* is a comprehensive study that shows both the Louis and the Vauban maquisards were overwhelmingly aged between 19 and 21.

The numbers of the Louis Maquis at Les Fréchots and those of the twelve armed groups in the villages, who were responsible for immediate action against small convoys and for early warning of enemy movement, amounted to 1,901 men, distributed as follows:

- 23 officers
- 1,440 men
- 1 mortar section (40 men)
- 1 bazooka section (40 men)
- 1 crack regiment (62 men)
- 2 groups of irregulars (40 men)
- 12 village groups (250 men)
- 6 doctors.

During the summer of 1944 alone, nine airdrops, sometimes performed with several large freight aircraft, prevented the maquis from running out of both weapons and munitions.

Intelligence and communications

Five radio suitcases allowed Baptist to communicate at all times with London for information on the development of fighting in France, and to ask for emergency air support against bigger German convoys crossing the Morvan.

Local telephone connections were also of paramount importance. At the post office in Luzy, all operators belonged to the Resistance. They remained in telephone contact with all the small towns on the roads leading to Autun. In this way, the movements of German troops could be made known early on and the maquis could organise its responses. When the troop movements were significantly larger, the RAF fighter-bombers were rapidly informed. This is how, on Sunday 3 September, we saw three planes decimate a large convoy, which was unable to escape via side roads because these had been mined by the maquis. Unfortunately, that day one of the aircraft was shot down.

A direct link was even secretly established between Captain Louis' office and Luzy's post office, taking advantage of a fire caused by the Resistance. During repairs, an additional line was covertly installed. As the Germans had a switch-board in the same office, one can imagine the difficulties faced by the operators in transmitting their information without being discovered.

There were also liaison officers; they were mostly women and, of course, they exercised their talents using bicycles. The most famous among them, nicknamed "Red Courier", was 23 years old when she became Chief Liaison Officer of the Gondolier network reporting to the SOE. The lady from Morvan Yvonne Moreau, born Marceau, fulfilled extraordinary missions.

I must not forget that I too once undertook that mission when I first joined the maquis.

Treating the wounded

In June, a first infirmary was established at Les Fréchots in a wooden hut, similar to the one used by Captain Louis for his command post. These huts were stolen from the Young Workers' Camp set up by Vichy near our camp in 1942.

Soon after, Dr Bondoux, who examined Michel and I when we arrived at the maquis, had set up a larger infirmary in an old farmhouse nearby, because of the increasing number of wounded fighters. Meanwhile, a young assistant doctor and a male nurse had joined the maquis.

Very soon, this proved inadequate. The difficult battles at the end of August and in September soon made a proper hospital necessary. The nearby Château de Champlevrier was converted for this purpose. The two expeditions that we made to a German depot in Cercy-la-Tour (my grandmother's village) made it possible to set up 50 beds. Two surgeons from Autun (Dr Sauter and his wife) saved many lives there.

Other hospital cells existed in Morvan, and they could treat the wounded from all the different maquis. Dr Prochiantz's was one of the most remarkable.

These emergency response systems worked non-stop during the great battle of Autun, fought by General de Lattre de Tassigny's French armies, which had landed in the South of France. The general's son, aged 18, was seriously injured at Autun, and happened to be treated as an emergency by Dr Prochiantz's medical unit, which had been set up closer to the front in the Hôtel Guyard in Anost.

Thirty doctors and surgeons are reckoned to have been working with the Morvan maquis in September 1944.

Transport

A significant fleet of cars was able to carry 600 men simultaneously between the camp at Les Fréchots and places where fighting men were needed.

There were among others the legendary Citroën 11 CV, which could accommodate a maquisard with his weapons on each of its two front wings! More numerous, of course, were trucks of all sizes, and buses.

Everything was hidden under the forest trees, next to the camp. To make this possible, we had to fell a certain number of trees and dig parking spaces for each vehicle so that it could manoeuvre easily.

The vehicles used petrol, but there were also many gas-powered trucks that could easily be fed with wood chips or charcoal. Getting hold of petrol was difficult, given that there was a huge shortage in France at the time. We had to attack warehouses to get any, or take it from the Germans. Some of their tankers were most welcome.

The maquisards after the liberation of Burgundy

On 25 September 1944, during a final rally, the Louis Maquis was disarmed and disbanded. Captain Baptist addressed his maquisards in an emotional speech. At the moment of victory, he praised equally the men who joined the Resistance from its inception and those who enlisted much later. I remember that he was almost in tears when he spoke of the death of Captain Louis, assuring us that the names of the sixty-seven maquisards who died in combat would never be erased from our memories.

Baptist was right: across France, monuments perpetuate the memory of those who gave their lives in battle, uniting the 9,844 Resistance fighters shot by the Germans with the 19,816 civilians slaughtered mainly in reprisal for Resistance action.

In Luzy, in the Louis Maquis square (Place du Maquis Louis), a war memorial stands as a reminder of these sacrifices. There is one at Les Fréchots too.

When the Louis Maquis was disbanded, we had the opportunity to carry on fighting. Some joined the Morvan Regiment, consisting solely of former

Resistance fighters from the different maquis, and joined the 1st French Army. This regiment consisted of 2,100 men divided into three battalions, of which one was from the Nevers region. They fought initially under the command of their own officers, and with their own weapons. It was this regiment, reduced to two battalions as its losses were so severe, which had the honour of planting the French flag at the top of the Guebwiller mountain on 4 February 1945. It was then incorporated into the regular army, with the 27th Infantry Battalion, and crossed the Rhine on 16 April 1945, before reaching Austria at the time of the armistice.

Other maquisards were directly incorporated into General Leclerc's 2nd Armoured Division. This was the case of my friend Needle (aged 18) who reached Austria in "his" tank! Two other maquisards from the Révol Group, my friends Speedboat (aged 19) and Jim (aged 23), signed up for the SAS. Trained in Britain, they quickly qualified as paratroopers, before parachuting into Holland behind German lines around Arnhem. The enemy had managed to hold their position after the first great battle. The SAS were in charge of disrupting the launch sites for the V1s and V2s that were ravaging England. They only returned by a miracle. As the Allied troops who were to join them had been delayed, they had to wait several days without food, whilst standing up to the assault of the SS. Having finally run out of ammunition, they had no way out, but were miraculously saved by a regiment of Polish free fighters.

As for me, I did not follow my friend Michel, otherwise known as Speedboat, to England to join the SAS. I returned to Nevers, before going to Paris to pursue my studies at the Faculty of Sciences. But I remember, at the time, feeling as though I were "deserting"!

After the Liberation of France, the maquisards made up by far the largest part of the regular army. We must not forget that the fighting would continue for another 9 months.

They were highly valued soldiers, because these trained men could be deployed immediately. And most of them had already endured their baptism of fire. Over the whole of France, the number of resistants and maquisards who were amalgamated into the regular army, and who fought all the way to victory, is reckoned to stand at around 137,000 (according to Jacques Canaud).

Before the D–Day landings, General Leclerc de Hautecloque had said to his men: "We are going in. We want to meet up with the good French who are fighting inside their country the fight that we are engaged in outside. We salute those who have already taken up arms! Yes! We are all part of the same army, the army of Liberation!"

De Lattre de Tassigny was also warning his soldiers: "Think of those who have remained in France, who have fought an undercover, murderous and active fight. Tomorrow you will meet those who have risen, they are your

My friend of the Révol Group Michel Chevrier, alias Vedette (Speedboat). Michel enrolled in the SAS with Jim, after the dissolution of the Louis Maquis. Here he is photographed in Holland soon after he parachuted behind German lines and was rescued by Polish troops.

brothers; you will want nothing more than seeing them take their place in your ranks."

De Lattre perfectly succeeded in merging resistants, maquisards and his own army. It was fair to say that "The FFI units that crossed the Rhine were equal in courage and efficiency to experienced units. In the melding achieved by de Lattre de Tassigny, history shows a national army." De Lattre even said that it was his greatest victory.

Epilogue

As a conclusion to this painful but glorious epic, I would like to quote this tribute to the French resistants, taken from Pierre Brossolette's BBC broadcast in London on 22 September 1942, "The French speak to the French". The gratitude expressed here is aimed at Berthin, Bondoux, Lauroy, Moreau, Passard, Pautet, Perraudin, Perriault, Pinet, Thomas, Truchot, and many others

Christiane Amanpour of CNN (Chief International Correspondent) interviews Hubert Verneret on the beach in Saint-Clément-des-Baleines, which was fortified by the Germans, about the Resistance and Remembrance Day on 11 November. The interview was broadcast on Amanpour's Facebook page on 11 November 2016.

who risked their lives in the Morvan, as early as 1941, so that we could continue to live free.

> Next to you, amongst you, often without your knowing it, men are fighting and dying: men of the underground fight for Liberation. Killed, wounded, shot, arrested, tortured, continually chased out of their homes, often cut off from their families, the story of these fighters is all the more moving in that they have neither uniforms nor banners; their regiments have no flag, and the names of their battles are not written in golden letters on shimmering silk, but only in the wounded memories of their brothers who have survived. Salute them, for their glorious deaths are like those on ships where one does not only die in the open air on deck, but also in the squalid darkness of the holds. This is how the men of the underground battle for France fight and die. Pay tribute to them, people of France! They are the stokers of glory.

List of Names of Maquis Members

English	French
"Achilles"	*Achille*
"Alle" (Lieutenant)	*Alle*
"André" (Captain)	*André*
"Armand" (Lieutenant Botté)	*Armand*
"Baptist" (Captain – Kenneth Mackenzie)	*Baptiste*
"Bouquet" (Strauss)	*Strauss/Bouquet*
"Cargo"	*Cargo*
"Chin"	*Menton*
"Cloth"	*Drap*
"Constantin"	*Constantin*
"Cotton"	*Coton*
"Cruiser"	*Croiseur*
"Eel"	*Anguille*
"Henry" (Captain)	*Henry*
"Jim"	*Jim*
"Jules"	*Jules*
"Lace"	*Dentelle*
"Leon" (Lieutenant)	*Léon*
"Louis" (Captain – Paul Sarrette)	*Louis*
"Moreau" (Major Roche)	*Moreau*
"Needle"	*Aiguille*
"Philip" (Fairweather)	*Philip*
"Poet"	*Poète*
"Révol"	*Révolu*
"Rosario"	*Rosario*
"Silk"	*Soie*

"Speedboat" (Michel Chevrier)   *Vedette*
"Torpi"   *Torpilleur*
"Trystram" (Lieutenant)   *Trystram*
"Will" (Hubert Verneret)   *Volonté*
"Wool"   *Laine*

Maps

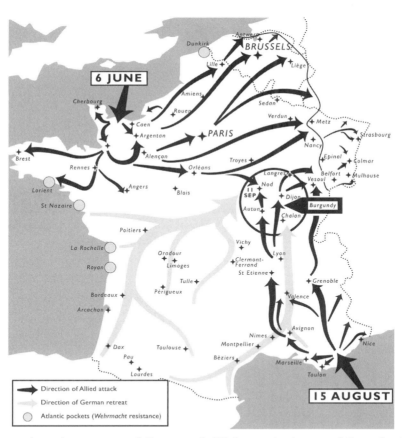

This map shows the movements of German and Allied troops in August and September 1944. The Germans passed through Burgundy during their withdrawal, though many German troops were trapped between the Allies, recently landed in Normandy, and the soldiers of General de Lattre de Tassigny, who landed in Provence on August 15. The Germans held four ports on the West Coast for a few months.

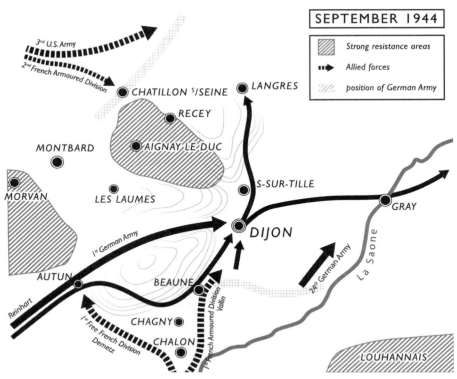

A huge clash of three armies took place on 8–10 September 1944 near Autun. The 1st German Army of General Reinhart was defeated by the 1st Division of the Free French of General de Lattre de Tassigny, with the assistance of Patton's 3rd U.S. Army and Leclerc's 2nd Armored Division, both coming from Normandy, and of Maquis Louis and the 18 other Maquis of Morvan. Casualties were enormous, and the Germans left behind 16,000 prisoners.